Queensurood !

CONTENTS

ORDERS OF SERVICE FOR HOLY COMMUNION

INTRODUCTION

Holy Communion, or the Lord's Supper, is the central act of Christian worship, in which the Church responds to our Lord's command, 'Do this in remembrance of me' (1 Corinthians 11:24-25).

Many of the themes of John and Charles Wesley's **Hymns on the Lord's Supper** (1745) are reflected in present-day ecumenical understanding of this sacrament. In communion with the people of God in heaven and on earth, we give thanks for God's mighty acts in creation and redemption, represented supremely in the life, death and resurrection of Jesus Christ. In this means of grace, the Church joyfully celebrates the presence of Christ in its midst, calls to mind his sacrifice and, in the power of the Holy Spirit, is united with him as the Body of Christ. At the Lord's table, Christ's disciples share bread and wine, the tokens of his dying love and the food for their earthly pilgrimage, which are also a foretaste of the heavenly banquet, prepared for all people. Those who gather around the table of the Lord are empowered for mission: apostles, sent out in the power of the Spirit, to live and work to God's praise and glory. One of the keynotes of the Methodist revival was John Wesley's emphasis on 'The Duty of Constant Communion' and it is still the duty and privilege of members of the Methodist Church to share in this sacrament. The Methodist Conference has encouraged local churches to admit baptized children to communion. Those who are communicants and belong to other Churches whose discipline so permits are also welcome as communicants in the Methodist Church.

The services of *Holy Communion* in this book are set out, after the initial 'The Gathering of the People of God', under the two historic headings, 'The Ministry of the Word' and 'The Lord's Supper'. The hinge point between the two is normally the sharing of the Peace. The shape of the Lord's Supper follows the record in scripture of Jesus' characteristic sharing with his disciples, especially after the final meal on the night before the crucifixion. His seven actions with the bread and wine (four with the bread, three with the wine) were taken up in the Church's tradition as a fourfold shape: Taking, Giving Thanks, Breaking and Sharing. In the Great Thanksgiving, the service of praise offered by God's people on earth is joined with the praises of the heavenly host, praising God, Father, Son and Holy Spirit. This Eucharistic Prayer (the word 'Eucharist', derived from a Greek word which means 'Thanksgiving', is increasingly accepted by Christians of all traditions as one of the names for this sacrament) is Trinitarian both in its structure and in its focus.

In this book, complete orders for **Holy Communion** have been provided for the major festivals and seasons, offering a wide range of seasonal language and imagery throughout each service. This also has the practical advantage that each service is complete in itself so that there is no need to turn to different parts of the book to find additional material. There are three orders for use in Ordinary Seasons (that is, when it is not a particular season or festival). Other sections of **The Methodist Worship Book** provide eucharistic prayers for certain specific occasions.

NOTES

1 The basic elements of each service are marked by the symbol *. Other sections may be omitted.

2 The term 'presiding minister' in these services means a presbyter or a person with an authorisation from the Conference to preside at the Lord's Supper. The presiding minister should begin and end the service. She/he should also greet the people at the Peace and preside over the fourfold Eucharistic action by taking the bread and wine, leading the Great Prayer of Thanksgiving, breaking the bread, and presiding over the sharing of the bread and wine. Other people may be invited to share in other parts of the service.

3 Several other services in this book are designed to take place within the context of *Holy Communion*. The **NOTES** for those services indicate the most appropriate places for their insertion into the service of *Holy Communion*.

4 In some churches it is customary to stand for the reading of the Gospel.

5 The juice of the grape shall be used.

6 What remains of the elements should be reverently consumed, or otherwise reverently disposed of, at the end of the service.

HOLY COMMUNION FOR ADVENT

NOTE

An Advent ceremony, such as the lighting of Advent candles, may be included after either no. 1 or no. 7, or at some other appropriate place.

THE GATHERING OF THE PEOPLE OF GOD

* 1 The presiding minister says:

> Grace and peace to you
> from God our Father and the Lord Jesus Christ.
> Blessèd are those who will come
> from east and west, from north and south,
> to feast in the kingdom of God.

2 Hymn

3   God of all glory,
> you brought the universe into existence,
> and raised up witnesses
> to your greatness and love.
> We praise and adore you.
> Grant that by the inspiration of your Holy Spirit
> we may worship and serve you,
> and praise your holy name;
> through Christ our Lord. **Amen.**

4 The commandments of the Lord Jesus may be read.

> Our Lord Jesus Christ said: 'The first commandment is, "Hear, O Israel: the Lord our God, the Lord is one; you shall love the Lord your God with all your heart, and with all your soul, and with all your mind, and with all your strength." The second is this, "You shall love your neighbour as yourself." There is no other commandment greater than these.' 'I give you a new commandment, that

you love one another. Just as I have loved you, you also
should love one another.'

Amen. Lord, have mercy.

* 5 The presiding minister says:

Let us confess our sins to God,
trusting in his mercy and forgiveness.

Holy and forgiving God,
we have sinned against you and each other
in thought and word and deed.
We have turned from your life-giving word,
and ignored the message of those you sent.
We are unprepared for the coming of your Son.
Have mercy upon us and forgive us,
that strengthened by your love
we may serve you more faithfully;
through Jesus Christ our Lord. Amen.

Silence

'I am making all things new,' says the Lord.

This is Christ's gracious word:

'Your sins are forgiven.'

Amen. Thanks be to God.

* 6 The collect of the day, or this or some other prayer:

God of mercy and power,
whose Son rules over all,
grant us so to live in obedience to your holy will,
that at his appearing
we may be raised to eternal life;
through Jesus Christ our Lord. **Amen.**

The collect of the Advent season (page 523) may also be said.

7 Hymn

OR *Benedictus*

Blessèd be the Lord, the God of Israel,
who has come to his people and set them free.

The Lord has raised up for us a mighty Saviour,
born of the house of his servant David.

Through the holy prophets, God promised of old
to save us from our enemies,
from the hands of all who hate us,
to show mercy to our forebears,
and to remember his holy covenant.

This was the oath God swore to our father Abraham:
to set us free from the hands of our enemies,
free to worship him without fear,
holy and righteous before him,
all the days of our life.

And you, child, shall be called the prophet of the
    Most High,
for you will go before the Lord to prepare his way,
to give his people knowledge of salvation
by the forgiveness of their sins.

In the tender compassion of our God
the dawn from heaven shall break upon us,
to shine on those who dwell in darkness and
    the shadow of death,
and to guide our feet into the way of peace.

Glory to the Father, and to the Son,
and to the Holy Spirit:
as it was in the beginning, is now,
and shall be for ever. Amen.

OR *Magnificat*

My soul proclaims the greatness of the Lord,
my spirit rejoices in God my Saviour,
who has looked with favour on his lowly servant.

**From this day all generations will call me blessèd:
the Almighty has done great things for me
and holy is his name.**

God has mercy on those who fear him,
from generation to generation.

**The Lord has shown strength with his arm
and scattered the proud in their conceit,
casting down the mighty from their thrones
and lifting up the lowly.**

God has filled the hungry with good things
and sent the rich away empty.

**He has come to the aid of his servant Israel,
to remember the promise of mercy,
the promise made to our forebears,
to Abraham and his children for ever.**

Glory to the Father, and to the Son,
and to the Holy Spirit:
**as it was in the beginning, is now,
and shall be for ever. Amen.**

THE MINISTRY OF THE WORD

*   Either two or three readings from scripture follow, the last of which is the Gospel.

8 Old Testament reading

9 A Psalm or portion of a Psalm may be said or sung.

10 Epistle

11 Hymn

*12   A reading from the Gospel according to . . .

Hear the Gospel of Christ.
Glory to Christ our Saviour.

The Gospel is read.

This is the Gospel of Christ.
Praise to Christ our Lord.

*13 Sermon

14 Hymn

*15 These or some other prayers of intercession:

Let us pray.

In joyful expectation of his coming to reign
we pray to our Lord, saying,
Come, Lord Jesus.

Come, Lord Jesus.

Come to your world as King of the nations.
We pray for . . .
Before you rulers will stand in silence.
Come, Lord Jesus.

Come, Lord Jesus.

Come to your Church as Lord and Judge.
We pray for . . .
Help us to live in the light of your coming
and give us a longing to do your will.
Come, Lord Jesus.

Come, Lord Jesus.

Come to your people
as Saviour and bearer of pain.
We pray for . . .
Enfold us all in your love and mercy,
wipe away the tears of failure, fear and distress,
and set us free to serve you for ever.
Come, Lord Jesus.

Come, Lord Jesus.

Come to us from heaven
with power and great glory,
and lift us up to meet you,
where with all your saints and angels,
we will live with you for ever.
Come, Lord Jesus.

Come, Lord Jesus. Amen.

16 Silence

THE LORD'S SUPPER

17 EITHER

Let us pray.

**We do not presume
to come to this your table,
merciful Lord,
trusting in our own
   righteousness,
but in your manifold
   and great mercies.
We are not worthy
so much as to gather up
   the crumbs under your
   table.
But you are the same Lord
whose nature is always to
   have mercy.
Grant us therefore,
   gracious Lord,
so to eat the flesh
of your dear Son Jesus
   Christ,
and to drink his blood,
that we may evermore
   dwell in him
and he in us. Amen.**

OR

We say together:

**Lord, we come to your
   table,
trusting in your mercy
and not in any goodness
   of our own.
We are not worthy
even to gather up
   the crumbs under your
   table,
but it is your nature
   always to have mercy,
and on that we depend.
So feed us
with the body and blood
of Jesus Christ, your Son,
that we may for ever
live in him and he in us.
Amen.**

18 The Peace

All stand.

May the God of peace make you holy
and keep you free from every fault
as you wait in joyful hope
for the coming of our Lord Jesus Christ.

The peace of the Lord be always with you.
And also with you.

The people may greet one another in the name of Christ.

THE PREPARATION OF THE GIFTS

19 Hymn

*20 The offerings of the people are presented. Bread and wine are brought to the table (or if already on the table are uncovered). The presiding minister takes the bread and wine and prepares them for use.

THE THANKSGIVING

*21 All stand.

The presiding minister leads the great prayer of thanksgiving:

The Lord be with you.
And also with you.

Lift up your hearts.
We lift them to the Lord.

Let us give thanks to the Lord our God.
It is right to give our thanks and praise.

God of all glory and light of our salvation,
we offer you thanks and praise
through Jesus Christ your Son our Lord.

By your living Word
you called all things into being,
breathed into life the desire of your heart
and shaped us in your own likeness.
Though we rejected your love,
you did not give us up
or cease to fashion our salvation.
You made a covenant to be our God,
spoke to us through the prophets,
and prepared the way for our redemption.

We praise you that in the fullness of time
you sent your only Son Jesus Christ.

The Lord of eternity,
announced by angels and born of Mary,
he became incarnate,
fulfilling the promise of your salvation.

And so we offer our praise
with all your people, on earth and in heaven.
With the full chorus of your creation,
we proclaim the glory of your name:

Holy, holy, holy Lord,
God of power and might,
heaven and earth are full of your glory,
Hosanna in the highest.
Blessèd is he who comes in the name of the Lord.
Hosanna in the highest.

We praise you, Lord God, King of the universe,
through our Lord Jesus Christ,
who, on the night in which he was betrayed,
took bread, gave thanks, broke it,
and gave it to his disciples, saying,
'Take this and eat it.
This is my body given for you.
Do this in remembrance of me.'

In the same way, after supper,
he took the cup, gave thanks,
and gave it to them, saying,
'Drink from it all of you.
This is my blood of the new covenant,
poured out for you and for many,
for the forgiveness of sins.
Do this, whenever you drink it,
in remembrance of me.'

Christ has died.
Christ is risen.
Christ will come in glory.
He is Alpha and Omega,
the beginning and the end;
the King of kings, and Lord of lords.

Recalling his death and resurrection,
and in obedience to his command,
we celebrate the offering of his eternal sacrifice,
until he comes again.

Through him, our Priest and King,
accept us as a living sacrifice,
a people for your praise.

Generous and holy God,
pour out your Spirit
that these gifts of bread and wine
may be for us the body and blood of Christ.

Refashion us in your image
that we may be found ready
at the coming of our Lord Jesus Christ.

**Blessing and honour and glory and power
be yours, O Lord, for ever and ever. Amen.**

*22 The Lord's Prayer

EITHER

We say together the prayer
that Jesus gave us:

**Our Father in heaven,
hallowed be your Name,
your kingdom come,
your will be done,
on earth as in heaven.
Give us today our daily
bread.
Forgive us our sins
as we forgive those who
sin against us.
Save us from the time of
trial
and deliver us from evil.
For the kingdom, the
power and the glory
are yours,
now and for ever. Amen.**

OR

As our Saviour taught his
disciples, we pray:

**Our Father, who art in
heaven,
hallowed be thy Name;
thy kingdom come;
thy will be done;
on earth as it is in heaven.
Give us this day our
daily bread.
And forgive us our
trespasses,
as we forgive those who
trespass against us.
And lead us not into
temptation;
but deliver us from evil.
For thine is the kingdom,
the power, and the
glory,
for ever and ever. Amen.**

THE BREAKING OF THE BREAD

*23 The presiding minister breaks the bread in the sight of the people in silence, or saying:

> The bread we break is a sharing in the body of Christ.
>
> The cup we take is a sharing in the blood of Christ.
>
> **Happy are those who share the banquet.**

OR

> Like those that look for the morning
> so our souls wait for the Lord.
>
> **Be known to us, Lord, in the breaking of the bread.**

*24 Silence, all seated or kneeling

THE SHARING OF THE BREAD AND WINE

*25 The presiding minister, those assisting with the distribution, and the people receive, according to local custom.

The presiding minister may say these or other words of invitation:

> The true bread of heaven gives life to the world.
> Come, all who are hungry, come and eat.
> Come, all who are thirsty, come and drink.

*26 Words such as the following are said during the distribution:

> The body of Christ keep you in eternal life. **Amen.**

> The blood of Christ keep you in eternal life. **Amen.**

27 During the distribution there may be appropriate music.

*28 The elements that remain are covered with a white cloth.

PRAYERS AND DISMISSAL

29 Silence

30   Let us pray.

**We thank you, Lord,
for feeding us with the bread of heaven
and the cup of salvation.
Keep us in your grace
and at the coming of Christ in glory
bring us with your saints
into the life of your kingdom. Amen.**

31 Hymn

32 The presiding minister says:

Christ the Sun of Righteousness
shine upon *you/us*
and prepare *your/our* hearts and souls
to meet him when he comes in glory;
and the blessing of God,
the Father, the Son and the Holy Spirit,
be *yours/ours*, now and always. **Amen.**

*33 The presiding minister says:

The day of the Lord is surely coming.
Be faithful in worship,
unwavering in hope,
fervent in the work of God's kingdom
and all the more as you see the Day drawing near.

Amen. Come, Lord Jesus.

HOLY COMMUNION
FOR CHRISTMAS AND EPIPHANY

NOTE

This service is intended for use between midnight on Christmas Eve and the Sunday after Epiphany inclusive.

THE GATHERING OF THE PEOPLE OF GOD

* 1 The presiding minister says:

> Great and wonderful are the things
> the Lord our God has done for us.
> The people who walked in darkness
> have seen a great light.

2 Hymn

3 In the silence and stillness
> let us open our hearts and lives to God,
> that we may be prepared for his coming
> as Light and Word, as Bread and Wine.

Silence

4 The presiding minister says:

> We say together:

> **Loving God,**
> **you have searched us and known us,**
> **our blindness, our frailties,**
> **our fears and our selfishness.**
> **In sorrow we confess**
> **that we have sinned against you**
> **and disobeyed your command to love.**
> **Forgive us,**
> **for the sake of your Son, Jesus Christ,**
> **who became like us**
> **that we might become like him. Amen.**

The true light that gives light to everyone
has come into the world.
To all who receive him,
he gives power to become children of God.
This is Christ's gracious word:

'Your sins are forgiven.'
Amen. Thanks be to God.

* 5 The collect of the day, or this or some other prayer:

Ever-living God,
whose glory was revealed
in the Word made flesh,
may we, who have seen such splendour
in the coming of your Son,
be true witnesses to your self-giving love in the world;
through Jesus Christ our Lord,
who is alive and reigns with you,
in the unity of the Holy Spirit,
one God, now and for ever. **Amen.**

6 EITHER *Glory to God in the highest*

**Glory to God in the highest,
and peace to God's people on earth.**

**Lord God, heavenly King,
almighty God and Father,
we worship you, we give you thanks,
we praise you for your glory.**

**Lord Jesus Christ, only Son of the Father,
Lord God, Lamb of God,
you take away the sin of the world:
have mercy on us.
You are seated at the right hand of the Father:
receive our prayer.**

For you alone are the Holy One,
you alone are the Lord,
you alone are the Most High, Jesus Christ,
with the Holy Spirit,
in the glory of God the Father. Amen.

OR *A Song of the Incarnation*

The grace of God has dawned upon the world
with healing for all.
The people who walked in darkness
have seen a great light:
Light has dawned upon us,
dwellers in a land as dark as death.
For a child has been born for us,
a son given to us.

God is love;
and his love was disclosed to us in this,
that he sent his only Son into the world to bring us life.
We know how generous our Lord Jesus Christ has
    been:
he was rich, yet for our sake he became poor,
so that through his poverty we might become rich.

God has spoken to us in the Son
whom he has made heir to the whole universe.
The Word became flesh and came to dwell among us.
We saw his glory,
such glory as befits the Father's only Son,
full of grace and truth.

THE MINISTRY OF THE WORD

*   Either two or three readings from scripture follow, the last of
which is the Gospel.

7   Old Testament reading

8   A Psalm or portion of a Psalm may be said or sung.

9 Epistle

10 Hymn

*11   A reading from the Gospel according to . . .

Hear the Gospel of Christ.
Glory to Christ our Saviour.

The Gospel is read.

This is the Gospel of Christ.
Praise to Christ our Lord.

*12 Sermon

13 Hymn

*14 These or some other prayers of intercession:

Let us pray.

Unlooked for,
Christ comes.

To shepherds,
watching their sheep through the long, dark night,
he comes with the glory of the angels' song
and in the humility of the manger.

Silence

Loving God, we pray for our community . . .
In the midst of our everyday lives, surprise us with
glimpses of the glorious, humble love at the heart of
existence.

Lord, come to your people.
In your mercy set us free.

Searched for,
Christ comes.

To the wise and powerful,
star-led to Bethlehem, seeking a king,
he comes, child of Mary,
crowned with meekness,
worthy of every gift.

Silence

Loving God, we pray for the leaders of the world . . .
Guide them with your light to the true wisdom of justice
and peace, of freedom and respect for every human life.

Lord, come to your people.
In your mercy set us free.

Longed for,
Christ comes.

To Anna and Simeon,
whose days are lived in faithful expectation,
he comes, a new life to the old,
a living prophecy of hope.

Silence

Loving God, we pray for the Church in all the world . . .
Unite us by your Spirit, and make us faithful witnesses to
the hope we have in you.

Lord, come to your people.
In your mercy set us free.

Prayed for,
Christ comes.

To men and women, girls and boys,
crying out in darkness, pain and loneliness,
he comes, baptized, at one with us,
our Saviour, healer and friend.

Silence

Loving God, we pray for those whose lives are hard and painful or whose existence is sorrowful, bitter or empty . . . In their need, may they know your healing touch, reaching out to comfort, strengthen and restore.

Lord, come to your people.
In your mercy set us free.

Unlooked for and searched for,
longed for and prayed for,
loving God, you come to us now
as you have come to your people in every age.
We thank you for all who have reflected the light of Christ.
Help us to follow their example
and bring us with them to eternal life;
through Jesus Christ our Lord. **Amen.**

*15 The Lord's Prayer

EITHER

We say together the prayer that Jesus gave us:

**Our Father in heaven,
hallowed be your Name,
your kingdom come,
your will be done,
on earth as in heaven.
Give us today our daily
  bread.
Forgive us our sins
as we forgive those who
  sin against us.
Save us from the time of
  trial
and deliver us from evil.
For the kingdom, the
  power and the glory
  are yours,
now and for ever. Amen.**

OR

As our Saviour taught his disciples, we pray:

**Our Father, who art in
  heaven,
hallowed be thy Name;
thy kingdom come;
thy will be done;
on earth as it is in heaven.
Give us this day our
  daily bread.
And forgive us our
  trespasses,
as we forgive those who
  trespass against us.
And lead us not into
  temptation;
but deliver us from evil.
For thine is the kingdom,
  the power, and the
  glory,
for ever and ever. Amen.**

16 The Peace

All stand.

Glory to God in the highest,
and on earth peace to all in whom he delights.

The peace of the Lord be always with you.
And also with you.

The people may greet one another in the name of Christ.

17 The Nicene Creed

All stand.

Let us profess the faith of the Church.

We believe in one God,
the Father, the Almighty,
maker of heaven and earth,
of all that is, seen and unseen.

We believe in one Lord, Jesus Christ,
the only Son of God,
eternally begotten of the Father,
God from God, Light from Light,
true God from true God,
begotten, not made,
of one Being with the Father;
through him all things were made.

For us and for our salvation
he came down from heaven,
was incarnate of the Holy Spirit and the Virgin Mary
and became truly human.
For our sake he was crucified under Pontius Pilate;
he suffered death and was buried.
On the third day he rose again
in accordance with the Scriptures;
he ascended into heaven
and is seated at the right hand of the Father.

He will come again in glory to judge the living and the
dead,
and his kingdom will have no end.

We believe in the Holy Spirit, the Lord, the giver of life,
who proceeds from the Father and the Son,
who with the Father and the Son is worshipped and
glorified,
who has spoken through the prophets.
We believe in one holy catholic and apostolic Church.
We acknowledge one Baptism for the forgiveness of
sins.
We look for the resurrection of the dead,
and the life of the world to come. Amen.

THE LORD'S SUPPER

THE PREPARATION OF THE GIFTS

18 Hymn

*19 The offerings of the people are presented. Bread and wine
are brought to the table (or if already on the table are
uncovered). The presiding minister takes the bread and wine
and prepares them for use.

20   Lord and Giver of every good thing,
we bring to you
bread and wine for our communion,
lives and gifts for your kingdom,
all for transformation through your grace and love,
made known in Jesus Christ our Saviour. **Amen.**

THE THANKSGIVING

*21 All stand.

The presiding minister leads the great prayer of thanksgiving:

The Lord be with you.
And also with you.

Lift up your hearts.
We lift them to the Lord.

Let us give thanks to the Lord our God.
It is right to give our thanks and praise.

Father, it is our joy and delight,
our reason for being,
to offer you thanks and praise.

All your actions show wisdom and love.
Through your Word you spoke creation into existence
and made us in your image and likeness.
When we disobeyed you and drew away from you,
you did not leave us in darkness
but sent your Son, the Word made flesh,
to be the light of the world.

Emptying himself of all but love,
he was born of Mary,
shared our human nature and died on the cross.

Yet you have raised him from death to eternal life;
and through him you have sent your holy and
    life-giving Spirit
to make us your people, a people of light,
to reflect your glory in all the earth.

And so with angels and archangels
and all the heavenly choir
we join in the unending hymn of praise:

Holy, holy, holy Lord,
God of power and might,
heaven and earth are full of your glory,
Hosanna in the highest.
Blessèd is he who comes in the name of the Lord.
Hosanna in the highest.

Holy and redeeming God,
we see your grace and truth in Jesus Christ our Lord,
who, on the night in which he was betrayed,
took bread, gave thanks, broke it,
and gave it to his disciples, saying,
'Take this and eat it.
This is my body given for you.
Do this in remembrance of me.'

In the same way, after supper,
he took the cup, gave thanks,
and gave it to them, saying,
'Drink from it all of you.
This is my blood of the new covenant,
poured out for you and for many,
for the forgiveness of sins.
Do this, whenever you drink it,
in remembrance of me.'

Christ is born.
The Saviour has come.
God is with us.

And so, Father, we remember and celebrate
all that Christ has done for us.
Send your Holy Spirit
that these gifts of bread and wine
may be for us the body and blood of Christ.

Through him we give ourselves to you.
May your Spirit draw us together
in the one body of Christ,
that we may have life in all its fullness,
live in your love,
and fill creation with a song of never-ending praise.

We ask this through your Son,
Jesus Christ our Lord.

**Through him, with him, and in him,
in the unity of the Holy Spirit,
all honour and glory be given to you,
almighty Father,
throughout all ages. Amen.**

THE BREAKING OF THE BREAD

*22 The presiding minister breaks the bread in the sight of the people in silence, or saying:

Christ is the bread of life.
Christ is the light of the world.

**God here among us,
light in the midst of us,
bring us light and life.**

*23 Silence, all seated or kneeling

THE SHARING OF THE BREAD AND WINE

*24 The presiding minister, those assisting with the distribution, and the people receive, according to local custom.

The presiding minister may say these or other words of invitation:

Christ is the true bread from heaven.
Whoever eats this bread will live for ever.

Draw near with faith.

*25 Words such as the following are said during the distribution:

The body of Christ given for you. **Amen.**

The blood of Christ shed for you. **Amen.**

26 During the distribution there may be appropriate music.

*27 The elements that remain are covered with a white cloth.

PRAYERS AND DISMISSAL

28 Silence

29   Let us pray.

**Father of all,
we give you thanks and praise,
that when we were still far off
you met us in your Son and brought us home.
Dying and living,
he declared your love, gave us grace, and opened the
      gate of glory.
May we who share Christ's body live his risen life;
we who drink his cup bring life to others;
we whom the Spirit lights give light to the world.
Keep us firm in the hope that you have set before us,
so we and all your children shall be free,
and the whole earth live to praise your name;
through Jesus Christ our Lord. Amen.**

30 Hymn

31 The presiding minister says:

May he, who by his incarnation
gathered into one things earthly and heavenly,
fill *your/our* lives with his light and joy and peace;
and the blessing of God,
the Father, the Son and the Holy Spirit,
remain with *you/us* always. **Amen.**

*32 The presiding minister says:

We go in the peace of Christ.

Thanks be to God.

HOLY COMMUNION
FOR ASH WEDNESDAY
(or for the First Sunday in Lent)

NOTES

1 This service is intended primarily for use on Ash Wednesday. Where this is not possible it may be used on the First Sunday in Lent.

2 The ceremony of ashes, a sign of repentance and a symbol of mortality, is an option within the service and, when included, is optional for members of the congregation.

3 It is customary, but not essential, to produce the ashes by burning the palm crosses of the previous year. This may be done before or during the service. The ashes should be placed in a bowl on or near the communion table.

THE GATHERING OF THE PEOPLE OF GOD

* 1 The presiding minister says:

Grace and peace to you from God our Father
and the Lord Jesus Christ.

2 Hymn

* 3 Sisters and brothers in Christ, since early days Christians have observed with great devotion the time of our Lord's passion, death and resurrection. It is the custom of the Church to prepare for this by a season of penitence and self-denial.

At first, this season of Lent was observed by those being prepared for Baptism at Easter and by those seeking restoration to the Church's fellowship. In the course of time, all Christians were invited to keep these days carefully, to take to heart the call to repentance, to receive the assurance of forgiveness proclaimed in the Gospel, and so to grow in faith and devotion to our Lord.

In the name of Christ, therefore, I invite you to observe this holy season of Lent, by prayer, self-denial and charitable giving; by self-examination and repentance; and by reading and meditating on God's word.

4 *Saviour of the World*

Jesus, Saviour of the world,
come to us in your mercy:
we look to you to save and help us.

By your cross and your life laid down
you set your people free:
we look to you to save and help us.

When they were ready to perish
you saved your disciples:
we look to you to come to our help.

In the greatness of your mercy
loose us from our chains:
forgive the sins of all your people.

Make yourself known
as our saviour and mighty deliverer:
save and help us that we may praise you.

Come now and dwell with us, Lord Christ Jesus:
hear our prayer and be with us always.

And when you come in your glory:
make us to be one with you
and to share the life of your kingdom.

* 5 This or some other Lenten collect:

Let us pray.

Almighty and merciful God,
you hate nothing that you have made,
and forgive the sins of all who are penitent.
Create in us new and contrite hearts,
so that when we turn to you
and confess our sins
we may receive
your full and perfect forgiveness;
through Jesus Christ our Lord. **Amen.**

THE MINISTRY OF THE WORD

*   In addition to the Psalm, either two or three readings from
scripture follow, the last of which is the Gospel.

6 Old Testament reading

* 7 Psalm 51 is said or sung:

**Have mercy on me, O God,
in your constant love;
in the fullness of your mercy
blot out my offences.
Wash away all my guilt,
and cleanse me from my sin.
Create in me a clean heart, O God,
and renew a right spirit within me.
Give me the joy of your help again
and strengthen me with a willing spirit.**

8 Epistle

9 Hymn

*10   A reading from the Gospel according to . . .

Hear the Gospel of Christ.
Glory to Christ our Saviour.

The Gospel is read.

This is the Gospel of Christ.
Praise to Christ our Lord.

*11 Sermon

12 The Ten Commandments

Hear the commandments
which God has given to his people:

I am the Lord your God;
you shall have no other gods besides me.

You shall not idolize anything God has made.

You shall not dishonour
the name of the Lord your God.

Remember the Lord's Day and keep it holy.

Lord, have mercy on us:
and turn our hearts to delight in your law.

Honour your father and your mother.

You shall not murder.

You shall not commit adultery.

You shall not steal.

You shall not give false evidence.

You shall not set your heart
on anything that is your neighbour's.

Lord, have mercy on us:
and turn our hearts to delight in your law.

THE ACT OF PENITENCE

*13 Silence

14   Let us pray.

Holy and merciful God,
we confess to you,
and to one another,
in communion with all the saints,
that we have sinned through our own fault
in thought, and word, and deed;
in what we have done
and in what we have failed to do.

We have not loved you with all our heart, soul, mind and
   strength.
We have not loved our neighbours as ourselves.
We have not loved one another as Christ has loved us.
We have not forgiven others as we have been forgiven.
We have grieved your Holy Spirit.

Lord, have mercy.
Christ, have mercy.

We confess to you, O God, all our past unfaithfulness:
the pride, hypocrisy and impatience of our lives,
our self-indulgence and our exploitation of other people.

Lord, have mercy.
Christ, have mercy.

We confess our preoccupation with worldly goods and
   comforts,
and our envy of others.

Lord, have mercy.
Christ, have mercy.

We confess our blindness to human need and suffering,
our indifference to injustice and cruelty,
our misuse and pollution of creation,
and our lack of concern for the generations to come.

Lord, have mercy.
Christ, have mercy.

We confess our negligence in prayer and worship,
and our failure to commend the faith that is in us.

Lord, have mercy.
Christ, have mercy.

*15 Silence

16 If there is to be an ashing ceremony, the presiding minister says:

Let us pray.

Almighty God,
you create us from the dust of the earth.
Let these ashes be for us
a sign of our repentance
and a symbol of our mortality.
May we always remember
that by your grace alone
we are given eternal life;
through Jesus Christ our Lord. **Amen.**

In the name of Christ,
I invite you to receive on your forehead
the sign of the cross.

The presiding minister first receives the sign of the cross in ash from an assistant. Those who wish come forward. At each signing these words are said:

Remember that you are dust and to dust you shall return.

Turn away from sin and be faithful to Christ.

During the ashing silence may be kept or there may be appropriate music.

*17 The presiding minister says:

<table>
<tr><td>EITHER</td><td>OR</td></tr>
</table>

EITHER	OR
The almighty and most merciful God grant you pardon, forgiveness of all your sins, time for true repentance and amendment of life, and the grace and comfort of the Holy Spirit. **Amen.**	May almighty God have mercy on us, forgive us our sins, and keep us in life eternal. **Amen.**

*18 The service continues from no. 15 in *Holy Communion for Lent and Passiontide* (page 152).

HOLY COMMUNION
FOR LENT AND PASSIONTIDE

THE GATHERING OF THE PEOPLE OF GOD

* 1 The presiding minister says:

Grace and peace to you from God our Father
and the Lord Jesus Christ.

2 Hymn

3 The commandments of the Lord Jesus may be read.

Our Lord Jesus Christ said: 'The first commandment is,
"Hear, O Israel: the Lord our God, the Lord is one; you
shall love the Lord your God with all your heart, and with
all your soul, and with all your mind, and with all your
strength." The second is this, "You shall love your
neighbour as yourself." There is no other commandment
greater than these.' 'I give you a new commandment, that
you love one another. Just as I have loved you, you also
should love one another.'

Amen. Lord, have mercy.

* 4 The presiding minister says:

Let us pray.

**Lord, you are steadfast in your love
and infinite in your mercy;
you welcome sinners
and invite them to be your guests.
We confess our sins,
trusting in you to forgive us.**

Silence

We have yielded to temptation and sinned:

Lord, have mercy.
Lord, have mercy.

We have turned from our neighbours in their need:

Christ, have mercy.
Christ, have mercy.

We have resisted your word in our hearts:

Lord, have mercy.
Lord, have mercy.

EITHER

The almighty and most
   merciful God
grant you pardon,
forgiveness of all your sins,
time for true repentance
and amendment of life,
and the grace and comfort
   of the Holy Spirit. **Amen.**

OR

May almighty God
have mercy on us,
forgive us our sins,
and keep us in life eternal.
Amen.

* 5 The collect of the day, or one of the following or some other prayer:

Until the Fifth Sunday in Lent:

Almighty God,
whose Son Jesus Christ
fasted forty days in the wilderness
and was tempted as we are, yet without sin:
give us grace to discipline ourselves
in obedience to your Spirit;
and, as you know our weakness,
so may we know your power to save;
through Jesus Christ our Lord. **Amen.**

From the Fifth Sunday in Lent:

Most merciful God,
who by the death and resurrection
of your Son Jesus Christ
delivered and saved the world:
grant that by faith in him
who suffered on the cross,
we may triumph in the power of his victory;
through Jesus Christ our Lord. **Amen.**

6 Hymn or *Saviour of the World*

Jesus, Saviour of the world,
come to us in your mercy:
we look to you to save and help us.

By your cross and your life laid down
you set your people free:
we look to you to save and help us.

When they were ready to perish
you saved your disciples:
we look to you to come to our help.

In the greatness of your mercy
loose us from our chains:
forgive the sins of all your people.

Make yourself known
as our saviour and mighty deliverer:
save and help us that we may praise you.

Come now and dwell with us, Lord Christ Jesus:
hear our prayer and be with us always.

And when you come in your glory:
**make us to be one with you
and to share the life of your kingdom.**

THE MINISTRY OF THE WORD

* Either two or three readings from scripture follow, the last of which is the Gospel.

7 Old Testament reading

8 A Psalm or portion of a Psalm may be said or sung.

9 Epistle

10 Hymn

*11 A reading from the Gospel according to . . .

Hear the Gospel of Christ.
Glory to Christ our Saviour.

The Gospel is read.

This is the Gospel of Christ.
Praise to Christ our Lord.

*12 Sermon

13 Affirmation of Faith: The Apostles' Creed

All stand.

**I believe in God, the Father almighty,
creator of heaven and earth.**

**I believe in Jesus Christ,
God's only Son, our Lord,
who was conceived by the Holy Spirit,
born of the Virgin Mary,
suffered under Pontius Pilate,
was crucified, died, and was buried;
he descended to the dead.
On the third day he rose again,
he ascended into heaven,
he is seated at the right hand of the Father,
and he will come to judge the living and the dead.**

I believe in the Holy Spirit,
the holy catholic Church,
the communion of saints,
the forgiveness of sins,
the resurrection of the body,
and the life everlasting. Amen.

14 Hymn

*15 These or some other prayers of intercession:

Let us pray for the Church of God throughout the world,
for . . . and for . . .

Lord, hear us.
Lord, graciously hear us.

Let us pray for those who have power and influence and
for all who govern the nations, for . . . and for . . .

Lord, hear us.
Lord, graciously hear us.

Let us pray for the powerless, for all victims of famine and
war, and for all who strive for justice and peace, for . . .
and for . . .

Lord, hear us.
Lord, graciously hear us.

Let us pray for the afflicted and sorrowful and for all who
need our prayers, for . . . and for . . .

Lord, hear us.
Lord, graciously hear us.

Let us remember before God those who have passed from
this life in faith and obedience, giving thanks for . . . and
for . . .

Lord, hear us.
Lord, graciously hear us.

Eternal God,
through the self-offering of your Son
you have filled our lives with your presence.
Help us in our sufferings and trials
and strengthen us in our weakness;
through Jesus Christ our Lord. **Amen.**

THE LORD'S SUPPER

16 The Peace

All stand.

In Christ, God was pleased to reconcile to himself all
things, whether on earth or in heaven, by making peace
through his blood which was shed on the cross.

The peace of the Lord be always with you.
And also with you.

THE PREPARATION OF THE GIFTS

17 Hymn

*18 The offerings of the people are presented. Bread and wine
are brought to the table (or if already on the table are
uncovered). The presiding minister takes the bread and wine
and prepares them for use.

THE THANKSGIVING

*19 All stand.

The presiding minister leads the great prayer of thanksgiving:

The Lord be with you.
And also with you.

Lift up your hearts.
We lift them to the Lord.

Let us give thanks to the Lord our God.
It is right to give our thanks and praise.

Blessing and praise belong to you,
gracious and eternal God.

Through your living Word
you created all things,
the majesty of the heavens
and the glory of the earth.
In your wisdom and goodness
you have made all people
in your image and likeness.

Therefore with saints and angels
and with all creation
we lift up our voices
to proclaim the glory of your name:

Holy, holy, holy Lord,
God of power and might,
heaven and earth are full of your glory.
Hosanna in the highest.
Blessèd is he who comes in the name of the Lord.
Hosanna in the highest.

Holy and gracious God,
we give you thanks and praise
that in the fullness of time
you gave your only Son
to share our human nature
and to be tempted in every way as we are,
yet without sin;
to set his face resolutely towards Jerusalem
and to be lifted high upon the cross,
that he might draw all creation to himself.

When the hour of his glory came,
and loving his own to the end,
he sat with them at supper,
took bread and, after giving thanks to you,
he broke it and gave it to his disciples, saying,
'Take, eat. This is my body which is for you.
Do this in remembrance of me.'

In the same way
he took the cup after supper, saying,
'Drink from this, all of you;
this cup is the new covenant in my blood.
Do this, whenever you drink it,
in remembrance of me.'

Dying, you destroyed our death.
Rising, you restored our life.
Lord Jesus, come in glory.

In obedience to his command
we recall his suffering and death,
his resurrection and ascension,
and we look for his coming in glory.

Send your Holy Spirit
that these gifts of bread and wine
may be for us the body and blood of Christ.

In union with Christ's offering for us,
we offer ourselves as a holy and living sacrifice.
Unite us in love and peace with all your people
until, with the whole company of heaven,
we are brought into the presence of your eternal glory,
through Jesus Christ our Lord.

Through him, with him, and in him,
in the unity of the Holy Spirit,
all honour and glory are yours,
almighty Father, now and for ever. Amen.

*20 The Lord's Prayer

EITHER

OR

We say together the prayer
that Jesus gave us:

As our Saviour taught his
disciples, we pray:

**Our Father in heaven,
hallowed be your Name,
your kingdom come,
your will be done,
on earth as in heaven.
Give us today our daily
bread.
Forgive us our sins
as we forgive those who
sin against us.
Save us from the time of
trial
and deliver us from evil.
For the kingdom, the
power and the glory
are yours,
now and for ever. Amen.**

**Our Father, who art in
heaven,
hallowed be thy Name;
thy kingdom come;
thy will be done;
on earth as it is in heaven.
Give us this day our
daily bread.
And forgive us our
trespasses,
as we forgive those who
trespass against us.
And lead us not into
temptation;
but deliver us from evil.
For thine is the kingdom,
the power, and the
glory,
for ever and ever. Amen.**

THE BREAKING OF THE BREAD

*21 The presiding minister breaks the bread in the sight of the
people in silence, or saying:

The bread we break is a sharing in the body of Christ.
Christ is the Bread of Life.

The presiding minister may lift the cup in silence, or saying:

The cup we take is a sharing in the blood of Christ.
Christ is the true Vine.

*22 Silence, all seated or kneeling

23   **Jesus, Lamb of God, have mercy on us.**
Jesus, bearer of our sins, have mercy on us.
Jesus, redeemer of the world, grant us peace.

24   EITHER   OR

Let us pray.   We say together:

We do not presume
to come to this your table,
merciful Lord,
trusting in our own
  righteousness,
but in your manifold
  and great mercies.
We are not worthy
so much as to gather up
  the crumbs under your
  table.
But you are the same
  Lord
whose nature is always to
  have mercy.
Grant us therefore,
  gracious Lord,
so to eat the flesh
of your dear Son Jesus
  Christ,
and to drink his blood,
that we may evermore
  dwell in him
and he in us. Amen.

Lord, we come to your
  table,
trusting in your mercy
and not in any goodness
  of our own.
We are not worthy
even to gather up
  the crumbs under your
  table,
but it is your nature
always to have mercy,
and on that we depend.
So feed us
with the body and blood
of Jesus Christ, your Son,
that we may for ever
live in him and he in us.
Amen.

THE SHARING OF THE BREAD AND WINE

*25 The presiding minister, those assisting with the distribution, and the people receive, according to local custom.

The presiding minister may say these or other words of invitation:

EITHER

Receive this holy sacrament
of the body and blood of Christ
and feed on the Lamb of God
with reverence and with faith.

OR

Come to this sacred table,
not because you must but because you may;
come, not to declare that you are righteous,
but that you desire to be true disciples of our Lord Jesus
    Christ:
come, not because you are strong,
but because you are weak;
not because you have any claim on heaven's rewards,
but because in your frailty and sin
you stand in constant need of heaven's mercy and help.

*26 Words such as the following are said during the distribution:

The body of Christ given for you. **Amen.**

The blood of Christ shed for you. **Amen.**

*27 The elements that remain are covered with a white cloth.

PRAYERS AND DISMISSAL

28 Silence

29 **Gracious God,**
we thank you that you have nourished us
with the bread of life
and with the cup of salvation.
May we who have received this sacrament
be strengthened in your service;
we who have sung your praises
live in your glory;
and we who have known
the greatness of your love
see you face to face in your kingdom;
through Jesus Christ our Lord. Amen.

30 Hymn

31 The presiding minister says:

The God of all grace
who has called *you/us* to eternal glory in Christ,
make *you/us* perfect,
confirming and strengthening *you/us;*
and to him be the power for ever and ever. **Amen.**

The almighty and merciful Lord,
the Father, the Son and the Holy Spirit,
bless *you/us* and keep *you/us*,
now and always. **Amen.**

*32 The presiding minister says:

Go in peace to love and serve the Lord.

In the name of Christ. Amen.

HOLY COMMUNION
FOR THE EASTER SEASON
(including ASCENSIONTIDE)

THE GATHERING OF THE PEOPLE OF GOD

* 1 The presiding minister says:

Alleluia! Christ is risen!
He is risen indeed! Alleluia!

or, from the Sixth Sunday of Easter:

Alleluia! The Lord reigns!
Let the earth rejoice! Alleluia!

2 Hymn

3   Let us pray.

Glory to you, O God:
you raised Jesus from the grave,
bringing us victory over death
and giving us eternal life.

Glory to you, O Christ:
for us and for our salvation
you overcame death
and opened the gate to everlasting life.

Glory to you, O Holy Spirit:
you lead us into the truth
and breathe new life into us.

Glory to you, Father, Son and Holy Spirit,
now and for ever. **Amen.**

4 The presiding minister says:

If we have fallen into despair,
Lord, forgive us.

If we have failed to hope in you,
Lord, forgive us.

If we have been fearful of death,
Lord, forgive us.

If we have forgotten the victory of Christ,
Lord, forgive us.

Silence

May the living God
raise *you/us* from despair,
give *you/us* victory over sin
and set *you/us* free in Christ. **Amen.**

* 5 The collect

On Easter Day:

Lord of all life and power,
who through the mighty resurrection of your Son
overcame the old order of sin and death
to make all things new in him:
grant that we, being dead to sin
and alive to you in Jesus Christ,
may reign with him in glory;
to whom with you in the unity of the Holy Spirit
be praise and honour, glory and might,
now and in all eternity. **Amen.**

On other days of the Easter season before the Sixth Sunday of
Easter, the collect of the day, or this or some other prayer:

Almighty God,
of your own free goodness and mercy
you have created us,
and through the resurrection
of your only-begotten Son
you have given us hope;
guard us by your love
and, in your wisdom, keep us in eternal life;
through Jesus Christ our Lord. **Amen.**

From the Sixth Sunday of Easter to the Saturday before
Pentecost, the collect of the day, or this or some other prayer:

Almighty God,
you have exalted your only Son, Jesus Christ,
with great triumph to your kingdom in heaven.
Mercifully give us faith
to know that, as he promised,
he abides with us on earth to the end of time,
who is alive and reigns
with you and the Holy Spirit,
one God now and for ever. **Amen.**

* 6 EITHER *Glory to God in the highest*

Glory to God in the highest,
and peace to God's people on earth.

Lord God, heavenly King,
almighty God and Father,
we worship you, we give you thanks,
we praise you for your glory.

Lord Jesus Christ, only Son of the Father,
Lord God, Lamb of God,
you take away the sin of the world:
have mercy on us.
You are seated at the right hand of the Father:
receive our prayer.

For you alone are the Holy One,
you alone are the Lord,
you alone are the Most High, Jesus Christ,
with the Holy Spirit,
in the glory of God the Father. Amen.

OR (before the Sixth Sunday of Easter) *A Song of Resurrection*

Christ our Passover has been sacrificed for us,
so let us celebrate the feast,

**not with the old leaven
of corruption and wickedness,
but with the unleavened bread
of sincerity and truth.**

Christ once raised from the dead dies no more;
death has no more dominion over him.

**In dying, he died to sin once for all;
In living, he lives to God.**

See yourselves therefore as dead to sin
and alive to God in Jesus Christ our Lord.

**Christ has been raised from the dead;
the first fruits of those who sleep.**

For as by one man came death,
by another has come also the resurrection of the dead.

**For as in Adam all die,
even so in Christ shall all be made alive.**

Glory to the Father, and to the Son,
and to the Holy Spirit:
**as it was in the beginning, is now,
and shall be for ever. Amen.**

OR (from the Sixth Sunday of Easter) *A Song of Christ's Glory*

**Christ Jesus was in the form of God,
but he did not cling to equality with God.**

He emptied himself,
taking the form of a servant,
and was born in our human likeness.
Being found in human form,
he humbled himself
and became obedient unto death,
even death on a cross.
Therefore, God has highly exalted him,
and bestowed on him the name above every name,
that at the name of Jesus every knee shall bow,
in heaven and on earth and under the earth,
and every tongue confess that Jesus Christ is Lord,
to the glory of God the Father.

OR a hymn

THE MINISTRY OF THE WORD

*   Either two or three readings from scripture follow, the last of which is the Gospel.

7 Reading from Acts or Old Testament reading

8 A Psalm or portion of a Psalm may be said or sung.

9 Epistle

10 Hymn

*11   A reading from the Gospel according to . . .

Alleluia! Hear the Gospel of Christ.
Glory to Christ our Saviour. Alleluia!

The Gospel is read.

Alleluia! This is the Gospel of Christ.
Praise to Christ our Lord. Alleluia!

*12 Sermon

13 Hymn

*14 These or some other prayers of intercession:

In the power of the resurrection we offer our prayers to God.

Let us pray.

Remember, O Lord, in your love
the Church throughout the world . . .
those recently baptized and confirmed . . .
those who minister to others . . .

Silence

May your whole Church know your power and be a sign that Christ is risen.

Lord of life,
hear us in your love.

Remember in your love the world you have made . . .
those who seek a fair and proper use of the world's resources . . .
those who strive for justice and peace among the nations . . .

Silence

May the whole earth be transformed by mercy and rejoice in hope.

Lord of life,
hear us in your love.

Remember in your love those who suffer . . .
the victims of violence and injustice . . .
those who mourn . . .

Silence

May all in need find comfort, strength and freedom in the living Christ.

Lord of life,
hear us in your love.

Remember in your love those who have died:
those who have confessed the faith
and those whose faith is known to you alone.

Silence

May all your children receive grace and light according to
their needs and come at last to share with all the saints in
life eternal.

Lord of life,
hear us in your love.

Gracious God, we ask these prayers through Jesus Christ,
our risen Lord and Saviour. **Amen.**

*15 The Lord's Prayer

EITHER

OR

We say together the prayer
that Jesus gave us:

As our Saviour taught his
disciples, we pray:

Our Father in heaven,
hallowed be your Name,
your kingdom come,
your will be done,
on earth as in heaven.
Give us today our daily
bread.
Forgive us our sins
as we forgive those who
sin against us.
Save us from the time of
trial
and deliver us from evil.
For the kingdom, the
power and the glory
are yours,
now and for ever. Amen.

Our Father, who art in
heaven,
hallowed be thy Name;
thy kingdom come;
thy will be done;
on earth as it is in heaven.
Give us this day our
daily bread.
And forgive us our
trespasses,
as we forgive those who
trespass against us.
And lead us not into
temptation;
but deliver us from evil.
For thine is the kingdom,
the power, and the
glory,
for ever and ever. Amen.

16 The Nicene Creed

All stand.

Let us profess the faith of the Church.

**We believe in one God,
the Father, the Almighty,
maker of heaven and earth,
of all that is, seen and unseen.**

**We believe in one Lord, Jesus Christ,
the only Son of God,
eternally begotten of the Father,
God from God, Light from Light,
true God from true God,
begotten, not made,
of one Being with the Father;
through him all things were made.
For us and for our salvation
he came down from heaven,
was incarnate of the Holy Spirit and the Virgin Mary
and became truly human.
For our sake he was crucified under Pontius Pilate;
he suffered death and was buried.
On the third day he rose again
in accordance with the Scriptures;
he ascended into heaven
and is seated at the right hand of the Father.
He will come again in glory to judge the living and the
    dead,
and his kingdom will have no end.**

**We believe in the Holy Spirit, the Lord, the giver of life,
who proceeds from the Father and the Son,
who with the Father and the Son is worshipped and
    glorified,
who has spoken through the prophets.
We believe in one holy catholic and apostolic Church.
We acknowledge one Baptism for the forgiveness of
    sins.
We look for the resurrection of the dead,
and the life of the world to come. Amen.**

THE LORD'S SUPPER

*17 The Peace

All stand.

The risen Christ came and stood among his disciples and said: 'Peace be with you!'

Then they were glad when they saw the Lord.

Alleluia! The peace of the risen Christ be always with you.
And also with you. Alleluia!

The people may greet one another in the name of the risen Lord.

THE PREPARATION OF THE GIFTS

18 Hymn

*19 The offerings of the people are presented. Bread and wine are brought to the table (or if already on the table are uncovered).

The presiding minister takes the bread and lifts it in the sight of the people, saying:

Here is bread, God's good gift.
It will become for us the bread of life.

The presiding minister takes the cup and lifts it in the sight of the people, saying:

Here is wine, God's good gift.
It will become for us the cup of salvation.

THE THANKSGIVING

*20 All stand.

The presiding minister leads the great prayer of thanksgiving:

The Lord be with you.
And also with you.

Lift up your hearts.
We lift them to the Lord.

Let us give thanks to the Lord our God.
It is right to give our thanks and praise.

Blessing and honour, glory and power,
are rightly yours, all-gracious God.
By your creative word
you brought the world to birth;
in your generous love
you made the human family,
that we might see your glory
and live for ever in your presence.

**Blessing and honour, glory and power,
are rightly yours, all-gracious God.**

When we wandered from you in our sin
you sought us with your steadfast love
and did not give us up.
In the fullness of time you sent your Son
to be our Saviour and Deliverer.
Made of flesh and blood, he lived our life
and died our death upon the cross.
Death could not hold him
and now he reigns at your right hand.

**Blessing and honour, glory and power,
are rightly yours, all-gracious God.**

Therefore with angels and archangels
and all the company of heaven
we bless and praise your glorious name, saying:

Holy, holy, holy Lord,
God of power and might,
heaven and earth are full of your glory,
Hosanna in the highest.
Blessèd is he who comes in the name of the Lord.
Hosanna in the highest.

Blessèd indeed is the Lord Jesus Christ
who, at supper with his friends,
took bread and gave you thanks,
broke it, gave it to them and said:
'Take this, all of you, and eat it.
This is my body given for you.
Do this in remembrance of me.'

When supper was ended,
he took the cup and gave you thanks,
gave it to them, and said:
'Drink from it all of you.
This is my blood of the new covenant,
poured out for you and for everyone,
for the forgiveness of sins.
Do this in remembrance of me.'

Dying, you destroyed our death.
Rising, you restored our life.
Lord Jesus, come in glory.

Therefore, Father,
we celebrate this Passover of gladness;
for as in Adam all die,
even so in Christ shall all be made alive.
Accept, through him, our great high priest,
this, our sacrifice of praise.

Send your Holy Spirit
that these gifts of bread and wine
may be for us the body and the blood of Christ.
Gather us, who share this feast,
into the kingdom of your glory
that with all your people in every time and place
we may praise and worship you for ever;
through Jesus Christ our Lord,

**by whom and with whom
in the unity of the Holy Spirit,
all honour and glory are yours,
heavenly Father, now and always. Amen.**

THE BREAKING OF THE BREAD

*21 The presiding minister breaks the bread in the sight of the
people in silence, or saying:

Alleluia! Christ our Passover is sacrificed for us.
Therefore let us keep the feast. Alleluia!

OR, after the Sixth Sunday of Easter:

The things of God for God's holy people.

**Jesus Christ is holy;
Jesus Christ is Lord.
Glory to God the Father.**

*22 Silence, all seated or kneeling

THE SHARING OF THE BREAD AND WINE

*23 The presiding minister, those assisting with the distribution,
and the people receive, according to local custom.

The presiding minister may say these or other words of
invitation:

We meet the risen Christ in the breaking of the bread.

Draw near with faith.

*24 Words such as the following are said during the distribution:

The body of Christ keep you in eternal life. **Amen.**

The blood of Christ keep you in eternal life. **Amen.**

25 During the distribution there may be appropriate music.

*26 The elements that remain are covered with a white cloth.

PRAYERS AND DISMISSAL

*27 Silence

28   Let us pray.

EITHER

A **God of our salvation,**
we thank you for our communion with the risen Christ
and with all who love him in earth and heaven.
We pray that, strengthened by his grace,
we may serve you faithfully all our days;
through Jesus Christ our Lord. Amen.

OR

B **Lord our God, we give you thanks**
because you have delivered us from the power of
darkness
and brought us into the kingdom of your Son.
Grant that, as by his resurrection
we are brought to new life,
so by his continued reign in us
we may be brought to eternal joy;
through the same Christ our Lord. Amen.

29 Hymn

30 The presiding minister says:

EITHER (before the Sixth Sunday of Easter)

A God the Father,
by whose glory Christ was raised from the dead,
strengthen *you/us*
to walk with him in his risen life;
and may almighty God bless *you/us*,
the Father, the Son and the Holy Spirit. **Amen.**

OR (from the Sixth Sunday of Easter)

B Christ our King
make *you/us* faithful and strong to do his will
that *you/we* may reign with him in glory;
and may almighty God bless *you/us*,
the Father, the Son and the Holy Spirit. **Amen.**

*31 The presiding minister says:

Alleluia!
Go in joy and peace to love and serve the Lord.

In the name of Christ. Alleluia!

HOLY COMMUNION
FOR THE DAY OF PENTECOST
and Times of Renewal in the Life of the Church

THE GATHERING OF THE PEOPLE OF GOD

* 1 The presiding minister says:

God declares:
I will pour out my Spirit on all flesh.
Then everyone who calls on the name of the Lord shall be
saved.

2 Hymn

3 Let us pray.

Come, Holy Spirit,
fill the hearts of your faithful people,
and kindle in us the fire of your love;
through Jesus Christ our Lord. Amen.

4 The presiding minister says:

Let us confess our sins to God.

Silence

Gracious and holy God,
we confess that we have sinned
against you and against our neighbour.
Your Spirit gives light,
but we have preferred darkness;
your Spirit gives wisdom,
but we have been foolish;
your Spirit gives power,
but we have trusted in our own strength.
For the sake of Jesus Christ, your Son,
forgive our sins,
and enable us by your Spirit
to serve you in joyful obedience,
to the glory of your Name. Amen.

There is now no condemnation
for those who live in union with Christ Jesus;
for the law of the Spirit of life
has set us free from the law of sin and death.

Amen. Thanks be to God.

* 5 The collect of the day, or this or some other prayer:

Faithful God,
you fulfilled the promise of Easter
by sending your Holy Spirit
and opening the way of eternal life
to all the human race.
Keep us in the unity of your Spirit,
that every tongue may tell of your glory;
through Jesus Christ our Lord,
who is alive and reigns with you,
in the unity of the Holy Spirit,
one God, now and for ever. **Amen.**

6 Hymn or *Glory to God in the highest*

Glory to God in the highest,
and peace to God's people on earth.

Lord God, heavenly King,
almighty God and Father,
we worship you, we give you thanks,
we praise you for your glory.

Lord Jesus Christ, only Son of the Father,
Lord God, Lamb of God,
you take away the sin of the world:
have mercy on us.
You are seated at the right hand of the Father:
receive our prayer.

For you alone are the Holy One,
you alone are the Lord,
you alone are the Most High, Jesus Christ,
with the Holy Spirit,
in the glory of God the Father. Amen.

THE MINISTRY OF THE WORD

* Either two or three readings from scripture follow, the last of which is the Gospel.

7 Old Testament reading or, on the Day of Pentecost, a reading from Acts.

8 A Psalm or portion of a Psalm may be said or sung.

9 Epistle

10 Hymn

*11 A reading from the Gospel according to . . .

Hear the Gospel of Christ.
Glory to Christ our Saviour.

The Gospel is read.

This is the Gospel of Christ.
Praise to Christ our Lord.

*12 Sermon

13 There may be a time of quiet reflection or testimony.

*14 These or some other prayers of intercession:

Gracious God,
whose Spirit helps us in our weakness
and guides us in our prayers,
we pray for the Church and for the world
in the name of Jesus Christ.

Renew the life and faith of the Church;
strengthen our witness;
and make us one in Christ . . .
Grant that we and all who confess that Christ is Lord
may be faithful in your service
and filled with the Spirit,
that the world may be turned to you.

Lord, in your mercy,
hear our prayer.

Guide the nations
in the ways of justice, liberty and peace;
and help them to seek
the unity and welfare of all people . . .
Give to all in authority
wisdom to know and strength to do what is right.

Lord, in your mercy,
hear our prayer.

Comfort those in sorrow;
heal the sick in body or in mind
and deliver the oppressed . . .
Grant us compassion for all who suffer,
and help us so to carry one another's burdens
that we may fulfil the law of Christ.

Lord, in your mercy,
hear our prayer.

Receive our thanks and praise
for all who have served you faithfully here on earth,
and especially those who have revealed to us
your grace in Christ . . .
May we and all your people
share the life and joy of your kingdom;
through Jesus Christ our Lord. **Amen.**

15 The Peace

All stand.

We are the Body of Christ.

In the one Spirit
we were all baptized into one body.
Let us therefore keep the unity of the Spirit
in the bond of peace.

The peace of the Lord be always with you.
And also with you.

The people may greet one another in the name of Christ.

16 The Nicene Creed

All stand.

Let us profess the faith of the Church.

**We believe in one God,
the Father, the Almighty,
maker of heaven and earth,
of all that is, seen and unseen.**

**We believe in one Lord, Jesus Christ,
the only Son of God,
eternally begotten of the Father,
God from God, Light from Light,
true God from true God,
begotten, not made,
of one Being with the Father;
through him all things were made.
For us and for our salvation
he came down from heaven,
was incarnate of the Holy Spirit and the Virgin Mary
and became truly human.**

**For our sake he was crucified under Pontius Pilate;
he suffered death and was buried.
On the third day he rose again
in accordance with the Scriptures;
he ascended into heaven
and is seated at the right hand of the Father.
He will come again in glory to judge the living and the
dead,
and his kingdom will have no end.**

**We believe in the Holy Spirit, the Lord, the giver of life,
who proceeds from the Father and the Son,
who with the Father and the Son is worshipped and
glorified,
who has spoken through the prophets.**

**We believe in one holy catholic and apostolic Church.
We acknowledge one Baptism for the forgiveness of
   sins.
We look for the resurrection of the dead,
and the life of the world to come. Amen.**

THE LORD'S SUPPER

THE PREPARATION OF THE GIFTS

17 Hymn

*18 The offerings of the people are presented. Bread and wine
   are brought to the table (or if already on the table are
   uncovered). The presiding minister takes the bread and wine
   and prepares them for use.

THE THANKSGIVING

*19 All stand.

   The presiding minister leads the great prayer of thanksgiving:

   The Lord be with you.
   And also with you.

   Lift up your hearts.
   We lift them to the Lord.

   Let us give thanks to the Lord our God.
   It is right to give our thanks and praise.

   It is indeed right,
   it is our duty and our joy,
   gracious and holy Father,
   always and everywhere to give you thanks.

   In the beginning
   your Spirit swept across the face of the waters,
   bringing order and beauty out of chaos.
   You formed us in your image
   and breathed into us the breath of life.

Though we turned away from you,
your love remained steadfast,
and you sent your only Son Jesus Christ
to be the Saviour of the world.

At his Baptism in the Jordan
he was anointed by your Spirit
and revealed as your beloved Son.
In the power of the Spirit
he was sent to preach good news to the poor,
to proclaim release to the captives
and recovery of sight to the blind,
to set at liberty those who are oppressed,
and to announce that the time had come
when you would save your people.

Sharing our human nature,
he died on the cross.
Raised again in glory,
he lives for ever to pray for us.
By the gift of the Spirit,
whom you have sent in his name,
you bring to completion the work of your Son,
leading us into all truth,
making us a people for your praise
and giving us power to proclaim the Gospel
in all the world.

And so, with all the faithful of every time and place,
we join with choirs of angels in the eternal hymn:

Holy, holy, holy Lord,
God of power and might,
heaven and earth are full of your glory.
Hosanna in the highest.
Blessèd is he who comes in the name of the Lord.
Hosanna in the highest.

On the night before he died,
the Lord Jesus took bread and gave you thanks.
He broke it, and gave it to his disciples, saying,
'Take, eat. This is my body, given for you.
Do this in remembrance of me.'

After supper, he took the cup of wine.
He gave thanks, and gave it to them, saying,
'Drink from it, all of you.
This is my blood of the new covenant,
poured out for all people
for the forgiveness of sins.
Do this in remembrance of me.'

And so,
in remembrance of all his mighty acts,
we offer you these gifts,
and with them ourselves
as a holy, living sacrifice.

You send forth your Spirit.
You bind us in love.
You renew the face of the earth.

Pour out your Holy Spirit
that these gifts of bread and wine
may be for us the body and blood of Christ.
Unite us with him and with one another
in mission to all the world;
and bring us with the whole creation
to your heavenly kingdom.

Through Christ, with Christ, in Christ,
in the unity of the Holy Spirit,
all blessing and honour and glory and power
be yours for ever and ever. Amen.

*20 The Lord's Prayer

EITHER

We say together the prayer
that Jesus gave us:

Our Father in heaven,
hallowed be your Name,
your kingdom come,
your will be done,
on earth as in heaven.
Give us today our daily
bread.
Forgive us our sins
as we forgive those who
sin against us.
Save us from the time of
trial
and deliver us from evil.
For the kingdom, the
power and the glory
are yours,
now and for ever. Amen.

OR

As our Saviour taught his
disciples, we pray:

Our Father, who art in
heaven,
hallowed be thy Name;
thy kingdom come;
thy will be done;
on earth as it is in heaven.
Give us this day our
daily bread.
And forgive us our
trespasses,
as we forgive those who
trespass against us.
And lead us not into
temptation;
but deliver us from evil.
For thine is the kingdom,
the power, and the
glory,
for ever and ever. Amen.

THE BREAKING OF THE BREAD

*21 The presiding minister breaks the bread in the sight of the
people in silence, or saying:

On the Day of Pentecost:

Alleluia! Christ our Passover is sacrificed for us.
Therefore let us keep the feast. Alleluia!

At other times:

We break this bread to share in the body of Christ.

Though we are many, we are one body,
because we all share in one bread.

*22 Silence, all seated or kneeling

THE SHARING OF THE BREAD AND WINE

*23 The presiding minister, those assisting with the distribution, and the people receive, according to local custom.

The presiding minister may say these or other words of invitation:

Receive this holy sacrament
of the body and blood of Christ,
and feed on the Lamb of God
with reverence and with faith.

*24 Words such as the following are said during the distribution:

The body of Christ keep you in eternal life. **Amen.**

The blood of Christ keep you in eternal life. **Amen.**

25 During the distribution there may be appropriate music.

*26 The elements that remain are covered with a white cloth.

PRAYERS AND DISMISSAL

27 Silence

28   Let us pray.

**God of power,
may the boldness of your Spirit transform us,
may the gentleness of your Spirit lead us,
and may the gifts of your Spirit equip us
to serve and worship you
now and always. Amen.**

29 Hymn

30 The presiding minister says:

The Spirit of truth lead *you/us* into all truth,
give *you/us* grace to confess that Jesus Christ is Lord,
and to proclaim the word and works of God;
and the blessing of God,
Spirit, Son and Father,
remain with *you/us* always. **Amen.**

*31 The presiding minister says:

We go into the world in the power of the Spirit
to fulfil our high calling as servants of Christ.

Thanks be to God. Amen.

HOLY COMMUNION
DURING ORDINARY SEASONS
(First Service)

NOTE

This service is intended for use (1) in the period which follows the Sunday after Epiphany and precedes Ash Wednesday and (2) in the period which follows the Day of Pentecost and precedes the First Sunday of Advent.

THE GATHERING OF THE PEOPLE OF GOD

* 1 The presiding minister reads a sentence of scripture.

2 Hymn

3   Let us pray.

Almighty God,
to whom all hearts are open,
all desires known,
and from whom no secrets are hidden:
cleanse the thoughts of our hearts
by the inspiration of your Holy Spirit,
that we may perfectly love you,
and worthily magnify your holy Name;
through Christ our Lord. Amen.

* 4 The presiding minister says:

Let us confess our sins to God.

Most merciful God,
we confess that we have sinned against you
in thought and word and deed.
We have not loved you with our whole heart.
We have not loved our neighbours as ourselves.

Silence

In your mercy,

**forgive what we have been,
help us to amend what we are,
and direct what we shall be;
that we may delight in your will
and walk in your ways;
through Jesus Christ our Lord. Amen.**

If we confess our sins,
God is faithful and just
and will forgive our sins,
and cleanse us from all unrighteousness.
Amen. Thanks be to God.

* 5 The collect of the day, or this or some other prayer:

Gracious God,
whose love for the world is revealed in your Son our
    Saviour:
grant that he may live in our hearts by faith,
and be proclaimed in our lives by love;
through the same Jesus Christ our Lord,
to whom with you and the Holy Spirit
be glory and praise, now and for ever. **Amen.**

6 *Glory to God in the highest,* a hymn, or some other canticle
of praise

**Glory to God in the highest,
and peace to God's people on earth.**

**Lord God, heavenly King,
almighty God and Father,
we worship you, we give you thanks,
we praise you for your glory.**

Lord Jesus Christ, only Son of the Father,
Lord God, Lamb of God,
you take away the sin of the world:
have mercy on us.
You are seated at the right hand of the Father:
receive our prayer.

For you alone are the Holy One,
you alone are the Lord,
you alone are the Most High, Jesus Christ,
with the Holy Spirit,
in the glory of God the Father. Amen.

THE MINISTRY OF THE WORD

*   Either two or three readings from scripture follow, the last of which is the Gospel.

7 Old Testament reading

8 A Psalm or portion of a Psalm may be said or sung.

9 Epistle

10 Hymn

*11   A reading from the Gospel according to . . .

Hear the Gospel of Christ.
Glory to Christ our Saviour.

The Gospel is read.

This is the Gospel of Christ.
Praise to Christ our Lord.

*12 Sermon

13 Hymn

*14 These or some other prayers of intercession:

Let us pray.

God, most gracious and most holy,
grant us the help of your Spirit
as we pray for the Church and the world.

We pray for the Church in every land . . .
for this church and for other local churches . . .
that we may worship and serve you
with reverence and joy.

Silence

Lord, hear us.
Lord, graciously hear us.

We pray for the peoples of the world . . .
and for the leaders of the nations . . .
that all may work together for justice and peace.

Silence

Lord, hear us.
Lord, graciously hear us.

We pray for those who are ill or distressed . . .
for the lonely and the bereaved . . .
and for those in any other need or trouble . . .
that they may be comforted and sustained.

Silence

Lord, hear us.
Lord, graciously hear us.

Father, we remember before you
all your servants who have died in the faith of Christ . . .

We pray that we too may lead faithful and godly lives in
this world,
and finally share with all the saints in everlasting joy;
through Jesus Christ our Lord. **Amen.**

*15 The Lord's Prayer

EITHER

We say together the prayer
that Jesus gave us:

**Our Father in heaven,
hallowed be your Name,
your kingdom come,
your will be done,
on earth as in heaven.
Give us today our daily
bread.
Forgive us our sins
as we forgive those who
sin against us.
Save us from the time of
trial
and deliver us from evil.
For the kingdom, the
power and the glory
are yours,
now and for ever. Amen.**

OR

As our Saviour taught his
disciples, we pray:

**Our Father, who art in
heaven,
hallowed be thy Name;
thy kingdom come;
thy will be done;
on earth as it is in heaven.
Give us this day our
daily bread.
And forgive us our
trespasses,
as we forgive those who
trespass against us.
And lead us not into
temptation;
but deliver us from evil.
For thine is the kingdom,
the power, and the
glory,
for ever and ever. Amen.**

16 The Peace

All stand.

We are the Body of Christ.

**In the one Spirit
we were all baptized into one body.
Let us therefore keep the unity of the Spirit
in the bond of peace.**

The peace of the Lord be always with you.
And also with you.

The people may greet one another in the name of Christ.

17 The Nicene Creed

All stand.

Let us profess the faith of the Church.

We believe in one God,
the Father, the Almighty,
maker of heaven and earth,
of all that is, seen and unseen.

We believe in one Lord, Jesus Christ,
the only Son of God,
eternally begotten of the Father,
God from God, Light from Light,
true God from true God,
begotten, not made,
of one Being with the Father;
through him all things were made.
For us and for our salvation
he came down from heaven,
was incarnate of the Holy Spirit and the Virgin Mary
and became truly human.
For our sake he was crucified under Pontius Pilate;
he suffered death and was buried.
On the third day he rose again
in accordance with the Scriptures;
he ascended into heaven
and is seated at the right hand of the Father.
He will come again in glory to judge the living and
**   the dead,**
and his kingdom will have no end.

We believe in the Holy Spirit, the Lord, the giver of life,
who proceeds from the Father and the Son,
who with the Father and the Son is worshipped and
**   glorified,**
who has spoken through the prophets.
We believe in one holy catholic and apostolic Church.

**We acknowledge one Baptism for the forgiveness of
sins.
We look for the resurrection of the dead,
and the life of the world to come. Amen.**

THE LORD'S SUPPER

THE PREPARATION OF THE GIFTS

18 Hymn

*19 The offerings of the people are presented. Bread and wine
are brought to the table (or if already on the table are
uncovered). The presiding minister takes the bread and wine
and prepares them for use.

20 Lord and Giver of every good thing,
we bring to you
bread and wine for our communion,
lives and gifts for your kingdom,
all for transformation through your grace and love,
made known in Jesus Christ our Saviour. **Amen.**

THE THANKSGIVING

*21 All stand.

The presiding minister leads the great prayer of thanksgiving:

The Lord be with you.
And also with you.

Lift up your hearts.
We lift them to the Lord.

Let us give thanks to the Lord our God.
It is right to give our thanks and praise.

We praise you, gracious Father,
our Maker and Sustainer.
You created the heavens and the earth
and formed us in your own image.
Though we sinned against you,
your love for us was constant,
and you sent your Son Jesus Christ
to be the Saviour of the world.

Sharing our human nature,
he was born of Mary
and baptized in the Jordan.
He proclaimed your kingdom, by word and deed,
and was put to death upon the cross.
You raised him from the dead;
you exalted him in glory;
and through him you have sent your Holy Spirit,
calling us to be your people,
a community of faith.

ON TRINITY SUNDAY

And now we give you thanks
because you have revealed your glory
as the glory of your Son and of the Holy Spirit:
three persons equal in majesty,
undivided in splendour,
yet one Lord, one God,
ever to be worshipped.
(And so . . .)

ON ALL SAINTS DAY (or for any saint)

And now we give you thanks
for the glorious pledge of the hope of our calling
which you have given us in your saints;
that, following their example
and strengthened by their fellowship,
we may run with perseverance
the race that is set before us,
and with them receive the unfading crown of glory.
(And so . . .)

And so, with angels and archangels
and all the choirs of heaven,
we join in the triumphant hymn:

Holy, holy, holy Lord,
God of power and might,
heaven and earth are full of your glory.
Hosanna in the highest.
Blessèd is he who comes in the name of the Lord.
Hosanna in the highest.

Holy God, we praise you
that on the night in which he was betrayed
our Saviour Christ took bread
and gave you thanks.
He broke it, and gave it to his disciples, saying,
'Take, eat. This is my body, given for you.
Do this in remembrance of me.'

After supper, he took the cup of wine,
gave thanks, and gave it to them, saying,
'Drink from it, all of you.
This is my blood of the new covenant,
poured out for all people
for the forgiveness of sins.
Do this in remembrance of me.'

Remembering, therefore, his death and resurrection,
and proclaiming his eternal sacrifice,
we offer ourselves to you in praise and thanksgiving,
as we declare the mystery of faith:

**Christ has died.
Christ is risen.
Christ will come again.**

Send down your Holy Spirit
that these gifts of bread and wine
may be for us the body and blood of Christ.
Unite us with him for ever
and bring us with the whole creation
to your eternal kingdom.

**Through Christ, with Christ, in Christ,
in the power of the Holy Spirit,
we worship you in songs of everlasting praise.
Blessing and honour and glory and power
be yours for ever and ever. Amen.**

THE BREAKING OF THE BREAD

*22 The presiding minister breaks the bread in the sight of the
people in silence, or saying:

EITHER

We break this bread to share in the body of Christ.

**Though we are many, we are one body,
because we all share in one bread.**

OR

The gifts of God for the people of God.
May Jesus Christ be praised!

*23 Silence, all seated or kneeling

24 EITHER

A Jesus, Lamb of God,
have mercy on us.
Jesus, bearer of our sins,
have mercy on us.
Jesus, redeemer of the world,
grant us peace.

OR

B Jesus is the Lamb of God
who takes away the sin of the world.
Happy are those who are called to his supper.

Lord, I am not worthy to receive you,
but only say the word and I shall be healed.

OR

C Let us pray.

We do not presume
to come to this your table, merciful Lord,
trusting in our own righteousness,
but in your manifold and great mercies.
We are not worthy
so much as to gather up the crumbs under your table.
But you are the same Lord
whose nature is always to have mercy.
Grant us therefore, gracious Lord,
so to eat the flesh of your dear Son Jesus Christ
and to drink his blood,
that we may evermore dwell in him
and he in us. Amen.

OR

D We say together:

**Lord, we come to your table,
trusting in your mercy
and not in any goodness of our own.
We are not worthy
even to gather up the crumbs under your table,
but it is your nature always to have mercy,
and on that we depend.
So feed us with the body and blood
of Jesus Christ, your Son,
that we may for ever live in him
and he in us. Amen.**

THE SHARING OF THE BREAD AND WINE

*25 The presiding minister, those assisting with the distribution, and the people receive, according to local custom.

The presiding minister may say these or other words of invitation:

Jesus said: 'I am the bread of life.
Those who come to me shall not hunger
and those who believe in me shall never thirst.'

Draw near with faith.

*26 Words such as the following are said during the distribution:

The body of Christ keep you in eternal life. **Amen.**

The blood of Christ keep you in eternal life. **Amen.**

27 During the distribution there may be appropriate music.

*28 The elements that remain are covered with a white cloth.

PRAYERS AND DISMISSAL

29 Silence

30 Let us pray.

**We thank you, Lord,
that you have fed us in this sacrament,
united us with Christ,
and given us a foretaste of the heavenly banquet
prepared for all people. Amen.**

31 This or some other hymn:

**Love's redeeming work is done,
Alleluia!
Fought the fight, the battle won;
Alleluia!
Vain the stone, the watch, the seal;
Alleluia!
Christ has burst the gates of hell;
Alleluia!**

**Soar we now where Christ has led,
Alleluia!
Following our exalted Head;
Alleluia!
Made like him, like him we rise;
Alleluia!
Ours the cross, the grave, the skies;
Alleluia!**

32 The presiding minister says:

The blessing of God,
the Father, the Son and the Holy Spirit,
remain with *you/us* always. **Amen.**

*33 The presiding minister says:

Go in peace in the power of the Spirit
to live and work to God's praise and glory.

Thanks be to God. Amen.

HOLY COMMUNION
DURING ORDINARY SEASONS
(Second Service)

NOTES

1 This service is intended for use (1) in the period which follows the Sunday after Epiphany and precedes Ash Wednesday and (2) in the period which follows the Day of Pentecost and precedes the First Sunday of Advent.

2 Musical settings other than those printed may be used.

THE GATHERING OF THE PEOPLE OF GOD

* 1 The presiding minister says:

God's grace and peace are with us.
Let our hearts be filled with joy.

2 Hymn

* 3 The presiding minister says:

Let us pray.

God of mercy,
your love for us is strong,
but our love for you is weak.
You call us to follow Jesus,
but we are slow to obey.
You care for all that you have made,
but we ignore the needs of others
and misuse your creation.
We are sorry for our sins.
Forgive us,
and help us to please you
by the way we live;
through Jesus Christ our Lord. Amen.

God is love
and forgives our sins through Jesus. **Amen.**

* 4 The collect of the day, or this or some other prayer:

Generous God,
you gave your Son for the life of the whole world.
Give us the joy of knowing the risen Christ,
and let your Holy Spirit guide us,
that we may love and serve you on earth
and live with you for ever in heaven;
through Jesus Christ our Lord. **Amen.**

5 Hymn or one of these versions of *Glory to God* or some other
act of praise

A

B **Glory to God in the highest,**
and peace to God's people on earth.

Lord God, heavenly King,
almighty God and Father,
we worship you, we give you thanks,
we praise you for your glory.

Lord Jesus Christ, only Son of the Father,
Lord God, Lamb of God,
you take away the sin of the world:
have mercy on us.
You are seated at the right hand of the Father:
receive our prayer.

For you alone are the Holy One,
you alone are the Lord,
you alone are the Most High, Jesus Christ,
with the Holy Spirit,
in the glory of God the Father. Amen.

THE MINISTRY OF THE WORD

*   Either two or three readings from scripture follow, the last of
    which is the Gospel.

6 Old Testament reading

7 A Psalm or portion of a Psalm may be said or sung.

8 Epistle

9 Hymn or Alleluia

Al - le - lu - ia,   Al - le - lu - ia,   Al- le- lu - ia!

*10   A reading from the Gospel according to . . .

Hear the Gospel of Christ.
Glory to Christ our Saviour.

The Gospel is read.

This is the Gospel of Christ.
Praise to Christ our Lord.

*11 Sermon

12 EITHER

A The Nicene Creed

All stand.

Let us profess the faith of the Church.

**We believe in one God,
the Father, the Almighty,
maker of heaven and earth,
of all that is, seen and unseen.**

**We believe in one Lord, Jesus Christ,
the only Son of God,
eternally begotten of the Father,
God from God, Light from Light,
true God from true God,
begotten, not made,
of one Being with the Father;
through him all things were made.
For us and for our salvation
he came down from heaven,
was incarnate of the Holy Spirit and the Virgin Mary
and became truly human.
For our sake he was crucified under Pontius Pilate;
he suffered death and was buried.**

On the third day he rose again
in accordance with the Scriptures;
he ascended into heaven
and is seated at the right hand of the Father.
He will come again in glory to judge the living and the
    dead,
and his kingdom will have no end.

We believe in the Holy Spirit, the Lord, the giver of life,
who proceeds from the Father and the Son,
who with the Father and the Son is worshipped and
    glorified,
who has spoken through the prophets.
We believe in one holy catholic and apostolic Church.
We acknowledge one Baptism for the forgiveness of
    sins.
We look for the resurrection of the dead,
and the life of the world to come. Amen.

OR

B An Affirmation of Faith

All stand.

Do you believe and trust in God the Father
who has created the universe?
We believe and trust in God the Father.

Do you believe and trust in Jesus, the Son of God,
who has redeemed the world?
We believe and trust in God the Son.

Do you believe and trust in the Holy Spirit,
who gives life to the people of God?
We believe and trust in God the Holy Spirit.

*13 Prayers of intercession

> for the universal Church,
> for peace and justice in the world,
> for those in authority,
> for the concerns of the local community,
> for those who suffer;
> thanksgiving for the departed.

A sung or spoken versicle and response may conclude each section.

THE LORD'S SUPPER

14 The Peace

All stand.

> Our Lord Jesus Christ said:
> 'I leave you peace, my peace I give to you.'
>
> The peace of the Lord be always with you.
> **And also with you.**

The people may greet one another in the name of Christ.

THE PREPARATION OF THE GIFTS

15 Hymn

*16 The offerings of the people are presented. Bread and wine are brought to the table (or if already on the table are uncovered). The presiding minister takes the bread and wine and prepares them for use.

THE THANKSGIVING

*17 All stand.

The presiding minister leads the great prayer of thanksgiving:

> The Lord be with you.
> **And also with you.**

Lift up your hearts.
We lift them to the Lord.

Let us give thanks to the Lord our God.
It is right to give our thanks and praise.

God our Father and our Mother,
we give you thanks and praise
for all that you have made,
for the stars in their splendour
and the world in its wonder
and for the glorious gift of human life.
With the saints and angels in heaven
we praise your holy name.

EITHER

A **Holy, holy, holy Lord,**
God of power and might,
heaven and earth are full of your glory.
Hosanna in the highest.
Blessèd is he who comes in the name of the Lord.
Hosanna in the highest.

OR
B

Ho - ly, ho - ly, ho - ly is the Lord;

1.
ho - ly is the Lord God al - migh - ty!

2.
ty! Who was, and is, and is to come!

Ho - ly ho-ly, ho - ly is the Lord!____

Holy God, you go on loving us
even when we turn away from you.
You sent your Son Jesus
who healed those who were sick,
wept with those who were sad,
and forgave sinners.
To show the world your love
he died for all upon the cross
and you raised him up in glory.

On the night before Jesus died,
he had supper with his disciples.
He took bread,
thanked you, as we are thanking you,
broke the bread,
and gave it to them, saying,
'Take, eat. This is my body, given for you.
Do this to remember me.'

**Jesus the Lord says, I am the bread,
the bread of life for the world am I.**

After supper, he took a cup of wine,
thanked you,
and gave it to his disciples, saying,
'Drink from it, all of you.
This cup is the new covenant in my blood.
It will be shed for you and for all people
for the forgiveness of sins.
Do this to remember me.'

**Jesus the Lord says, I am the vine,
the true and fruitful vine am I.**

And so, God of love,
we remember that Jesus died and rose again
to make all things new.
Through his offering for us all,
we offer our whole life to you in thanks and praise.

Send your Holy Spirit
that these gifts of bread and wine
may be for us Christ's saving body and blood.
May this same Spirit unite us
with all your people on earth and in heaven.

Bring us at last
to live in your glory with all your saints,
that we may praise you for ever,
through Jesus your Son,
in the fellowship of the Holy Spirit.

This or some other doxology ending with **Amen** is sung or said:

**All glory to the Father be,
the Spirit and the Son:
all glory to the One in Three
while endless ages run.
Alleluia! Amen.**

*18 The Lord's Prayer

EITHER

OR

We say together the prayer
that Jesus gave us:

As our Saviour taught his
disciples, we pray:

**Our Father in heaven,
hallowed be your Name,
your kingdom come,
your will be done,
on earth as in heaven.
Give us today our daily
bread.
Forgive us our sins
as we forgive those who
sin against us.
Save us from the time of
trial
and deliver us from evil.
For the kingdom, the
power and the glory
are yours,
now and for ever. Amen.**

**Our Father, who art in
heaven,
hallowed be thy Name;
thy kingdom come;
thy will be done;
on earth as it is in heaven.
Give us this day our
daily bread.
And forgive us our
trespasses,
as we forgive those who
trespass against us.
And lead us not into
temptation;
but deliver us from evil.
For thine is the kingdom,
the power, and the
glory,
for ever and ever. Amen.**

THE BREAKING OF THE BREAD

*19 The presiding minister breaks the bread in the sight of the
people in silence, or saying:

The bread we break is a sharing in the body of Christ.
Christ is the Bread of life.

The presiding minister may lift the cup in silence, or saying:

The cup of blessing for which we give thanks
is a sharing in the blood of Christ.
Christ is the true Vine.

*20 Silence, all seated or kneeling

21   Jesus, Lamb of God,
      have mercy on us.
      Jesus, bearer of our sins,
      have mercy on us.
      Jesus, redeemer of the world,
      grant us peace.

THE SHARING OF THE BREAD AND WINE

*22 The presiding minister, those assisting with the distribution,
     and the people receive, according to local custom.

     Appropriate words of invitation may be said.

*23 Words such as the following are said during the distribution:

      The body of Christ, given for you. **Amen.**

      The blood of Christ, shed for you. **Amen.**

24 During the distribution there may be appropriate music.

*25 The elements that remain are covered with a white cloth.

PRAYERS AND DISMISSAL

26 Silence

27   Let us pray.

      God of glory,
      we have seen with our eyes
      and touched with our hands
      the bread of heaven.
      Strengthen us in our life together
      that we may grow in love
      for you and for each other;
      through Jesus Christ our Lord. Amen.

28 Hymn

29 The presiding minister says:

> The blessing of God,
> the Father, the Son and the Holy Spirit,
> be upon *you/us*, now and always. **Amen.**

*30 The presiding minister says:

> Go in peace to love and serve the Lord.
>
> **In the name of Christ. Amen.**

HOLY COMMUNION
DURING ORDINARY SEASONS
(Third Service)

NOTE

This service is intended for use (1) in the period which follows the Sunday after Epiphany and precedes Ash Wednesday and (2) in the period which follows the Day of Pentecost and precedes the First Sunday of Advent.

THE GATHERING OF THE PEOPLE OF GOD

* 1 The presiding minister says:

> The grace of the Lord Jesus Christ,
> and the love of God,
> and the fellowship of the Holy Spirit,
> be with you all. **Amen.**

2 Hymn

3 Let us pray.

> **Give us, O God, a vision of your glory,**
> **that we may worship you in spirit and in truth,**
> **and offer the praise of glad and thankful hearts;**
> **through Christ our Lord. Amen.**

* 4 The presiding minister says:

> Let us call to mind our sins.

> Silence

Lord Jesus, you came into the world to save sinners:

Lord, have mercy.
Lord, have mercy.

We have brought sorrow and hurt to you,
to others and to ourselves:

Christ, have mercy.
Christ, have mercy.

You give yourself to heal and renew us,
and to bring us strength:

Lord, have mercy.
Lord, have mercy.

EITHER	OR
May almighty God	Know that your sins
have mercy on us,	are forgiven
forgive us our sins,	through Jesus Christ,
and keep us in life eternal.	our Saviour,
Amen.	and rejoice in his goodness
	and grace.
	Amen.
	Thanks be to God.

* 5 The collect of the day, or this or some other prayer:

God, the source of all wisdom,
you teach us in your word
that love is the fulfilling of the law:
grant that we may love you with all our heart
and our neighbours as ourselves;
through Jesus Christ our Lord. **Amen.**

6 Hymn or *You are Worthy* or a short time of praise

You are worthy, our Lord and God;
to receive glory and honour and power,
for you have created all things:
and by your will they were created and have their
being.

You are worthy, O Christ,
for you were slain:
and with your blood
you redeemed the human race for God,
and have chosen us to be a holy priesthood
from every people and nation.
To the One who is seated on the throne
and to the Lamb:
be blessing and honour, glory and might,
for ever and ever. Amen.

THE MINISTRY OF THE WORD

* Either two or three readings from scripture follow, the last of which is the Gospel.

7 Old Testament reading

8 A Psalm or portion of a Psalm may be said or sung.

9 Epistle

10 Hymn

*11 A reading from the Gospel according to . . .

Hear the Gospel of Christ.
Glory to Christ our Saviour.

The Gospel is read.

This is the Gospel of Christ.
Praise to Christ our Lord.

*12 Sermon

13 There may be a time of quiet reflection or testimony.

14 Hymn

*15 These or some other prayers of intercession:

In faith let us pray to God our Father,
in the name of his Son, Jesus Christ,
and in the power of the Holy Spirit.

God of love, we pray for the life of your Church throughout the world . . . May every congregation be a community of love and every Christian a witness to your grace. Renew all who worship in this place that we may be a living fellowship in your Spirit and serve our neighbourhood.

Your kingdom come.
Your will be done.

God of mercy, we pray for the life of the world . . . and for those who exercise power . . . Show us how to live as members of the human family; to reject the ways of war; to bear each other's burdens and to work together for justice and peace.

Your kingdom come.
Your will be done.

God of compassion, we pray for those who are ill or anxious at home or in hospital . . . We pray for those whose lives are filled with fear and despair . . . Draw near with your saving love and bring healing and hope.

Your kingdom come.
Your will be done.

God of glory, we rejoice in the communion of saints; we remember all who have faithfully lived and all who have died in Christian hope, especially . . . Help us to follow their example and bring us with them into the fullness of your eternal joy.

Your kingdom come.
Your will be done.

Merciful God,
you have prepared for those who love you
such good things as pass our understanding;
pour into our hearts such love towards you
that we, loving you above all things,
may obtain your promises,
which exceed all that we can desire;
through Jesus Christ our Lord. **Amen.**

THE LORD'S SUPPER

16 The Peace

   All stand.

   Our Lord Jesus Christ said to the apostles:
   'I leave you peace, my peace I give to you.'

   The peace of the Lord be always with you.
   And also with you.

   The people may greet one another in the name of Christ.

THE PREPARATION OF THE GIFTS

17 Hymn

*18 The offerings of the people are presented. Bread and wine
    are brought to the table (or if already on the table are
    uncovered). The presiding minister takes the bread and wine
    and prepares them for use.

THE THANKSGIVING

*19 All stand.

   The presiding minister leads the great prayer of thanksgiving:

   The Lord be with you.
   And also with you.

   Lift up your hearts.
   We lift them to the Lord.

Let us give thanks to the Lord our God.
It is right to give our thanks and praise.

It is indeed right, always and everywhere,
to give thanks to you, the true and living God.
Endless is your mercy and eternal is your reign.
All creation rejoices in your radiant splendour.

You made a covenant with your people
and declared your purpose of justice and love.
When all things were ready,
you sent your Son to be our Saviour.
In words and deeds he proclaimed your kingdom,
and obeyed your will even to death on the cross.

Through his mighty resurrection
he overcame sin and death
to set the whole creation free.

Therefore with saints and angels
and with all the choirs of heaven,
we join in the song of eternal praise:

Holy, holy, holy Lord,
God of power and might,
heaven and earth are full of your glory.
Hosanna in the highest.
Blessèd is he who comes in the name of the Lord.
Hosanna in the highest.

We praise you, Father,
that on the night in which he was betrayed,
our Lord Jesus took bread and gave thanks,
broke it, and gave it to his disciples, saying,
'Take and eat. This is my body, given for you.
Do this in remembrance of me.'

After supper, he took the cup, gave thanks,
and gave it for all to drink, saying,
'This cup is the new covenant of my blood,
shed for you and for all people
for the forgiveness of sin.
Do this in remembrance of me.'

As often as we eat this bread and drink this cup
we proclaim the Lord's death until he comes.

Therefore, gracious God,
with this bread and this cup
we remember that our Lord offered his life for us.

Believing the witness of his resurrection and ascension,
we look for his coming in glory,
and our sharing in his great and promised feast.
Amen. Come, Lord Jesus.

Send now, we pray, your Holy Spirit,
that these gifts of bread and wine
may be for us the body and blood of Christ
and that we may live to your praise and glory
with all your saints in light.
Amen. Come, Holy Spirit.

Join our prayers
and the prayers of all your people
on earth and in heaven
with the intercession of Christ,
our great high priest,

through whom, with whom, and in whom,
in the unity of the Holy Spirit,
all worship and honour are yours,
almighty God and Father,
for ever and ever. Amen.

*20 The Lord's Prayer

EITHER	OR
We say together the prayer that Jesus gave us:	As our Saviour taught his disciples, we pray:
Our Father in heaven, hallowed be your Name, your kingdom come, your will be done, on earth as in heaven. Give us today our daily bread. Forgive us our sins as we forgive those who sin against us. Save us from the time of trial and deliver us from evil. For the kingdom, the power and the glory are yours, now and for ever. Amen.	**Our Father, who art in heaven, hallowed be thy Name; thy kingdom come; thy will be done; on earth as it is in heaven. Give us this day our daily bread. And forgive us our trespasses, as we forgive those who trespass against us. And lead us not into temptation; but deliver us from evil. For thine is the kingdom, the power, and the glory, for ever and ever. Amen.**

THE BREAKING OF THE BREAD

*21 The presiding minister breaks the bread in the sight of the people in silence, or saying:

The bread we break is a sharing in the body of Christ.
Christ is the Bread of Life.

The presiding minister may lift the cup in silence, or saying:

The cup we take is a sharing in the blood of Christ.
Christ is the True Vine.

*22 Silence, all seated or kneeling

23 *Lamb of God* or some other short hymn or song on a similar
theme

> Jesus, Lamb of God,
> **have mercy on us.**
> Jesus, bearer of our sins,
> **have mercy on us.**
> Jesus, redeemer of the world,
> **grant us peace.**

THE SHARING OF THE BREAD AND WINE

* 24 The presiding minister, those assisting with the distribution,
and the people receive, according to local custom.

The presiding minister may say these or other words of
invitation:

> Jesus is the Lamb of God
> who takes away the sin of the world.
> Happy are those who are called to his supper.

> Receive the body of Christ which was given for you
> and the blood of Christ which was shed for you,
> and feed on him in your hearts,
> by faith with thanksgiving.

*25 Words such as the following are said during the distribution:

> The body of Christ. **Amen.**

> The blood of Christ. **Amen.**

26 During the distribution there may be appropriate music.

*27 The elements that remain are covered with a white cloth.

PRAYERS AND DISMISSAL

28 Silence

29   Let us pray.

**We praise you, God,
for the bread of heaven
and the cup of salvation
which you give for the life of the world.
With this food for our journey
bring us with your saints
to the feast of your glory. Amen.**

30 Hymn

31 The presiding minister says:

EITHER

OR

The Lord bless you and
  keep you;
the Lord make his face to
  shine on you
and be gracious to you;
the Lord look on you with
  kindness
and give you peace. **Amen.**

God be gracious to us
  and bless us,
and make his face to shine
  upon us. **Amen.**

*32 The presiding minister says:

Go in peace to love and serve the Lord.

In the name of Christ. Amen.

GUIDANCE FOR ORDERING A SERVICE
OF HOLY COMMUNION

THE GATHERING OF THE PEOPLE OF GOD

The presiding minister and the people gather in God's name.
Notices may be given and news items may be shared.
Acts of approach and praise are offered in song and prayer.
A prayer of penitence is followed by an assurance of God's forgiveness.

There may be a brief introduction to the service.
A short prayer reflecting the season or festival is offered.

THE MINISTRY OF THE WORD

The scriptures are read, concluding with a passage from the Gospels.
God's word is proclaimed and shared in songs, hymns, music, dance and other art forms, in a sermon, or in comment, discussion and in silence.

Prayers are offered for the Church, for the world and for those in need; a remembrance is made of those who have died; and the Lord's Prayer may be said.

THE LORD'S SUPPER

The Peace is introduced by an appropriate sentence of scripture and may be shared by the presiding minister and the people.

The offerings of the people may be placed on the Lord's table.

The presiding minister takes the bread and wine and prepares them for use.

The presiding minister leads the great prayer of thanksgiving:

The people are invited to offer praise to God.
There is thanksgiving
for creation,
for God's self-revelation,
for the salvation of the world through Christ,
and for the gift of the Holy Spirit,
with special reference to the season or festival.

God's glory may be proclaimed in a version of 'Holy, holy, holy'.

The story of the institution of the Lord's Supper is told.
Christ's death and resurrection are recalled.
God is asked to receive the worshippers' sacrifice of praise.

There is prayer for the coming of the Holy Spirit that the gifts of bread and wine may be, for those who are participating, the body and blood of Christ.

The worshippers, offering themselves in service to God, ask to be united in communion with all God's people on earth and in heaven.

The prayer concludes with all honour and glory being given to God, the Father, the Son and the Holy Spirit, the people responding with a loud '**Amen**'.

The Lord's Prayer is said, if it has not been said earlier.

The presiding minister breaks the bread in silence, or saying an appropriate sentence.

The presiding minister and people receive communion, after which the elements that remain are covered.

PRAYERS AND DISMISSAL

A short prayer is offered in which the worshippers thank God for the communion and look forward to the final feast in God's kingdom.

There may be a time of praise.

The presiding minister says a blessing and sends the people out to live to God's praise and glory.

HOLY COMMUNION IN A HOME
OR A HOSPITAL

NOTES

1 This service is a celebration of *Holy Communion* and should be distinguished from the order for *Extended Communion*, during which elements already set aside at a previous celebration of *Holy Communion* are received.

2 For pastoral reasons, it may sometimes be desirable to give communion by dipping the bread lightly in the wine or to give only the bread or the wine. Bread dipped in wine is given with the words, 'The body and blood of Christ, given for you'.

3 If necessary, the words printed in **bold** type may be said by the presiding minister alone.

---

1 The peace of the Lord be always with you.
And also with you.

2 Let us pray.

Almighty God,
to whom all hearts are open,
all desires known,
and from whom no secrets are hidden:
cleanse the thoughts of our hearts
by the inspiration of your Holy Spirit,
that we may perfectly love you,
and worthily magnify your holy Name;
through Christ our Lord. Amen.

3   Let us confess our sins to God.

Most merciful God,
we have sinned in thought, word and deed,
and in what we have left undone.
For the sake of your Son, Jesus Christ,
have mercy on us and forgive us,
that we may serve you in newness of life,
to the glory of your name. Amen.

God our Father,
who forgives all who truly repent,
have mercy on *you/us,*
pardon and deliver *you/us* from all *your/our* sins,
confirm and strengthen *you/us* in all goodness,
and keep *you/us* in eternal life;
through Jesus Christ our Lord. **Amen.**

*   4   The collect of the day or some other prayer

*   5   One or more short readings from scripture, including a passage from the Gospels

6   A brief exposition may be given.

7   A short act of intercession

*   8   The Lord's Prayer

EITHER	OR
We say together the prayer that Jesus gave us:	As our Saviour taught his disciples, we pray:
Our Father in heaven, **hallowed be your Name,** **your kingdom come,** **your will be done,** **on earth as in heaven.** **Give us today our daily** **bread.** **Forgive us our sins** **as we forgive those who** **sin against us.**	**Our Father, who art in** **heaven,** **hallowed be thy Name;** **thy kingdom come;** **thy will be done;** **on earth as it is in heaven.** **Give us this day our** **daily bread.** **And forgive us our** **trespasses,**

Save us from the time of trial
and deliver us from evil.
For the kingdom, the power and the glory are yours,
now and for ever. Amen.

as we forgive those who trespass against us.
And lead us not into temptation;
but deliver us from evil.
For thine is the kingdom, the power, and the glory,
for ever and ever. Amen.

* 9 The presiding minister takes the bread and wine and prepares them for use.

*10 The presiding minister leads the great prayer of thanksgiving:

The Lord be with you.
And also with you.

Lift up your hearts.
We lift them to the Lord.

Let us give thanks to the Lord our God.
It is right to give our thanks and praise.

Father, almighty and everliving God,
it is right to give you thanks and praise
at all times and in all places.
With angels and archangels
and with all your people on earth and in heaven,
we proclaim your glorious name,
evermore praising you and saying:

Holy, holy, holy Lord,
God of power and might,
heaven and earth are full of your glory.
Hosanna in the highest.
Blessèd is he who comes in the name of the Lord.
Hosanna in the highest.

Holy and blessèd God,
you have created all things
and made us in your own image.
When we had fallen into sin
you gave your only Son Jesus Christ
to suffer death upon the cross for our redemption,
making there the one perfect sacrifice
for the sins of the whole world.

On the night that he was betrayed he took bread;
and when he had given you thanks,
he broke it, and gave it to his disciples, saying,
'Take, eat. This is my body which is given for you.
Do this in remembrance of me.'

In the same way, after supper, he took the cup;
and when he had given you thanks,
he gave it to them, saying,
'Drink this, all of you.
This is my blood of the new covenant
which is shed for you and for many
for the forgiveness of sins.
Do this, as often as you drink it,
in remembrance of me.'

Therefore, Father,
we do as Christ your Son commanded;
we remember his passion and death,
we celebrate his resurrection and ascension,
and we look for the coming of his kingdom.

Accept through him
this our sacrifice of praise and thanksgiving;
and grant that by the power of your life-giving Spirit,
we who eat and drink these holy gifts
may share in the body and blood of Christ
and be united with all your people
on earth and in heaven;

through the same Jesus Christ our Lord,
by whom, and with whom,
in the unity of the Holy Spirit,
all honour and glory are yours,
almighty Father,
for ever and ever. **Amen.**

*11   The presiding minister breaks the bread in silence, or saying:

The bread we break is a sharing in the body of Christ.

The cup we take is a sharing in the blood of Christ.

*12   Silence

13   EITHER   OR

Let us pray.   We say together:

**We do not presume
to come to this your table,
merciful Lord,
trusting in our own
    righteousness,
but in your manifold
    and great mercies.
We are not worthy
so much as to gather up
    the crumbs under your
    table.
But you are the same Lord
whose nature is always to
    have mercy.
Grant us therefore,
    gracious Lord,
so to eat the flesh
of your dear Son Jesus
    Christ,
and to drink his blood,
that we may evermore
    dwell in him
and he in us. Amen.**

**Lord, we come to your
    table,
trusting in your mercy
and not in any goodness
    of our own.
We are not worthy
even to gather up
    the crumbs under your
    table,
but it is your nature
    always to have mercy,
and on that we depend.
So feed us
with the body and blood
of Jesus Christ, your Son,
that we may for ever
live in him and he in us.
Amen.**

*14 Bread and wine are given with these or similar words:

The body of our Lord Jesus Christ, given for you. **Amen.**

The blood of our Lord Jesus Christ, shed for you. **Amen.**

15 Silence

16 EITHER

A Let us pray.

We thank you, Lord,
that you have fed us in this sacrament,
united us with Christ,
and given us a foretaste of the heavenly banquet
prepared for all people. Amen.

OR

B Lord our God,
you have strengthened us for our journey
with Christ, the Living Bread.
Bring us to be with you in glory
that with angels and archangels
and all the company of heaven
we may praise you for ever. **Amen.**

*17 The peace of God
which passes all understanding,
keep *your/our* hearts and minds
in the knowledge and love of God
and of his Son, Jesus Christ our Lord;
and the blessing of God,
the Father, the Son and the Holy Spirit,
remain with *you/us* always. **Amen.**

EXTENDED COMMUNION

NOTES

1 This service is an act of worship during which the participants receive elements previously set apart at a service of *Holy Communion*.

2 This service may be led by a presbyter, or by a deacon stationed in the circuit, or by a lay person with an authorisation from the Conference to preside at the Lord's Supper, or by a lay person duly prepared and trained for the purpose who has been so appointed by the local Church Council in accordance with Standing Orders.

3 The setting apart of bread and wine in the service of public worship takes place when all have communicated. That which is set apart should be placed in a home communion set or other suitable vessels provided by the Church Council, before the cloth is placed over the rest of the elements, and should be taken from the communion table to a safe place where it can be kept until the time when it is to be taken to a home or hospital.

4 It is desirable that communion in a home or hospital using this Order should be given on the same day as the bread and wine have been set apart. When it is known that this will not be possible and there will be some delay, consideration should be given to the setting apart of some of the bread in the form of wafers for use in the home or hospital.

5 For pastoral reasons, it may sometimes be desirable to give communion by dipping the bread lightly in the wine or to give only the bread or the wine. Bread dipped in wine is given with the words, 'The body and blood of Christ, given for you'.

6 If necessary, the words printed in **bold** type may be said by the leader alone.

7 The scripture reading(s) at no. 7 may appropriately be selected from among those which were used at the service of Holy Communion at which the elements were set apart.

* 1 The bread and wine are reverently set out.

* 2   Grace to you and peace from God our Father
and the Lord Jesus Christ. **Amen**.

3 The following may be said:

The Church of God, to which we belong, has taken bread
and wine and given thanks over them according to our
Lord's command. I bring these holy gifts that you may
share in the communion of his body and blood. The bread
and wine which we share in this service come from a
celebration of the Lord's Supper at *N* . . . Church on *(date)*.
We who are many are one body, because we all share in
one bread.

4   Let us pray.

Almighty God,
to whom all hearts are open,
all desires known,
and from whom no secrets are hidden:
cleanse the thoughts of our hearts
by the inspiration of your Holy Spirit,
that we may perfectly love you,
and worthily magnify your holy Name;
through Christ our Lord. Amen.

5   Let us confess our sins to God.

Most merciful God,
we have sinned in thought, word and deed,
and in what we have left undone.
For the sake of your Son, Jesus Christ,
have mercy on us and forgive us,
that we may serve you in newness of life,
to the glory of your name. Amen.

God our Father, who forgives all who truly repent,
have mercy on *you/us,*
pardon and deliver *you/us* from all *your/our* sins,
confirm and strengthen *you/us* in all goodness,

and keep *you/us* in eternal life;
through Jesus Christ our Lord. **Amen.**

* 6 God our Father,
we come to this feast which you have prepared,
as guests whom you have invited:
may we receive the bread of eternal life
which you provide for our healing and strength;
through Christ our Lord. **Amen.**

* 7 One or more short readings from scripture, including a
passage from the Gospels

8 A brief exposition may be given.

9 These or some other prayers of thanksgiving and intercession
may be said:

We praise you, God our Father,
for creating all things
and for sending your Son Jesus Christ
to be our Saviour.
We give you thanks
for the outpouring of your Holy Spirit,
for our life together in your Church
and for our calling to serve you in the world.
Yours, Lord, is the greatness and the power,
the majesty and the splendour,
now and for ever. **Amen.**

Let us pray for the whole Church of God in Christ Jesus,
and for peace and justice throughout the world.

Appropriate concerns may be mentioned here, and may
include reference to the life of the local church.

Lord God, make your ways known upon earth,
and your saving power among all peoples.

Renew your Church in holiness,
and help us to serve you with joy.

Guide the leaders of this and every nation,
that justice may prevail throughout the world.

Bless and strengthen the sick and the suffering,
and grant us your salvation.

Make us one with the apostles and martyrs,
and bring us with your saints to glory everlasting.

We ask these prayers in the name of our Lord and Saviour
Jesus Christ. **Amen.**

*10 The Lord's Prayer

EITHER

OR

We say together the prayer
that Jesus gave us:

As our Saviour taught his
disciples, we pray:

**Our Father in heaven,
hallowed be your Name,
your kingdom come,
your will be done,
on earth as in heaven.
Give us today our daily
    bread.
Forgive us our sins
as we forgive those who
    sin against us.
Save us from the time of
    trial
and deliver us from evil.
For the kingdom, the
    power and the glory
    are yours,
now and for ever. Amen.**

**Our Father, who art in
    heaven,
hallowed be thy Name;
thy kingdom come;
thy will be done;
on earth as it is in heaven.
Give us this day our
    daily bread.
And forgive us our
    trespasses,
as we forgive those who
    trespass against us.
And lead us not into
    temptation;
but deliver us from evil.
For thine is the kingdom,
    the power, and the
    glory,
for ever and ever. Amen.**

11   EITHER   OR

Let us pray.	We say together:
We do not presume to come to this your table, merciful Lord, trusting in our own righteousness, but in your manifold and great mercies. We are not worthy so much as to gather up the crumbs under your table. But you are the same Lord whose nature is always to have mercy. Grant us therefore, gracious Lord, so to eat the flesh of your dear Son Jesus Christ, and to drink his blood, that we may evermore dwell in him and he in us. Amen.	**Lord, we come to your table, trusting in your mercy and not in any goodness of our own. We are not worthy even to gather up the crumbs under your table, but it is your nature always to have mercy, and on that we depend. So feed us with the body and blood of Jesus Christ, your Son, that we may for ever live in him and he in us. Amen.**

*12 These or other words of invitation:

Receive this holy sacrament in remembrance that Christ died for you, and feed on him in your heart by faith with thanksgiving.

Bread and wine are given with these or similar words:

The body of Christ, given for you. **Amen.**

The blood of Christ, shed for you. **Amen.**

13 EITHER

A Let us pray.

We thank you, Lord,
that you have fed us in this sacrament,
united us with Christ,
and given us a foretaste of the heavenly banquet
prepared for all people. Amen.

OR

B Lord our God,
you have strengthened us for our journey
with Christ, the Living Bread.
Bring us to be with you in glory
that with angels and archangels
and all the company of heaven
we may praise you for ever. **Amen.**

*14   The peace of God
which passes all understanding,
keep *your/our* hearts and minds
in the knowledge and love of God
and of his Son, Jesus Christ our Lord;
and the blessing of God,
the Father, the Son and the Holy Spirit,
remain with *you/us* always. **Amen.**

ACKNOWLEDGEMENTS

Every effort has been made to ensure that the following list of acknowledgements is as comprehensive as possible, but the experience of those involved in the preparation of **The Methodist Worship Book** is similar to that of the compilers of the **Book of Common Order** of the Church of Scotland, who state:

> Many sources have contributed to the compilation of this book, and not all of them are now traceable. Individual members of the Committee prepared drafts, which were revised more or less drastically by the Committee, often resulting in final versions which looked little like the original drafts. Among the casualties of this sometimes protracted process was the identity of many of the sources; they could not be recalled, nor did there seem to be any way to track them down. The Panel wishes to record at once both its indebtedness to any who may recognise in this book rhythms and patterns, expressions and phrases, ideas and images which are their own, and its regret that it became impossible to ask permission or seek consent for their inclusion . . .

> If, through inadvertence, copyright material has been used without permission or acknowledgement, the publisher will be grateful to be informed and will be pleased to make the necessary correction in subsequent editions.

The symbol * in the following paragraphs denotes that a text has been altered.

Except where indicated below, all psalms, scripture readings and scripture sentences are taken from **The New Revised Standard Version of the Bible (Anglicized Edition),** © 1989, 1995 by the Division of Christian Education of the National Council of Churches of Christ in the United States of America, and are used by permission. All rights reserved.

Some scripture sentences are from **The Revised Standard Version,** © 1946 and 1952 by the Division of Christian Education of the National Council of Churches of Christ in the United States of America, and are used by permission. All rights reserved.

Some scripture sentences are from **The Revised English Bible,** © 1989 Oxford University Press and Cambridge University Press.

One scripture sentence comes from **The New Jerusalem Bible,** © 1985 Darton Longman & Todd and Doubleday & Co. Inc.

The text* of Psalm 51 on page 143 appears in **A New Zealand Prayer Book – He Karakia Mihinare o Aotearoa,** © 1989 The Provincial Secretary, the Church of the Province of New Zealand. This book is also the source of one scripture sentence.

The texts of *Glory to God in the highest,* the Nicene Creed, the Apostles' Creed, *Sursum Corda, Sanctus, Benedictus Qui Venit, Gloria Patri, Te Deum Laudamus, Benedictus, Magnificat* and the left hand column version of the Lord's Prayer are from **Praying Together,** © 1988 by the English Language Liturgical Commission (ELLC).

The introduction to the Peace on page 168 is from **Lent, Holy Week and Easter,** © 1984, 1986 The Central Board of Finance of the Church of England. Reproduced by permission.

The seasonal introductions to the blessing* on page 184, the prayer, 'We do not presume . . .', on pages 123, 157, 195, 227 and 233, the post-communion prayer on page 140, the preface for Trinity Sunday* on page 192 and one scripture sentence are extracts from **The Alternative Service Book 1980,** © 1980 The Central Board of Finance of the Church of England. Reproduced by permission.

The prayers* on pages 121f and the first part of the blessing* on page 128 are extracts from **The Promise of his Glory,** © 1990, 1991 The Central Board of Finance of the Church of England. Reproduced by permission.

The address* on pages 141f, and the prayer over the ashes* on page 146 are from **The Book of Common Prayer** of the Episcopal Church of the United States of America, 1979.

The act of penitence* on page 145f is from **The Book of Alternative Services,** © 1985 The General Synod of the Anglican Church of Canada.

Two lines of prayer B on page 172 are from David Silk, **Prayers for the Alternative Services,** Mowbray 1980, 1986.

The prayers* on pages 176f are from **A Book of Services,** © 1980 The United Reformed Church.

The prayer of confession* on pages 185f is from **The Daily Office Revised,** © 1978 The Joint Liturgical Group.

The preface for All Saints Day on page 193 is from **An Anglican Prayer Book 1989,** © 1989 The Provincial Trustees of the Church of the Province of Southern Africa.

The address* at no. 3 on page 230 is an extract from **Ministry to the Sick** © 1983 The Central Board of Finance of the Church of England. Reproduced by permission.